Indoor and Vertical Gardening

The Ultimate Guide to Growing Fruit, Herbs, Vegetables, and Flowers Indoors, and on a Living Wall along with Tips for Urban Gardens and Building a Container Garden

© Copyright 2021

The contents of this book may not be reproduced, duplicated, or transmitted without direct written permission from the author.

Under no circumstances will any legal responsibility or blame be held against the publisher for any reparation, damages, or monetary loss due to the information herein, either directly or indirectly.

Legal Notice:

You cannot amend, distribute, sell, use, quote, or paraphrase any part or the content within this book without the consent of the author.

Disclaimer Notice:

Please note the information contained within this document is for educational and entertainment purposes only. No warranties of any kind are expressed or implied. Readers acknowledge that the author is not engaging in the rendering of legal, financial, medical, or professional advice. Please consult a licensed professional before attempting any techniques outlined in this book.

By reading this document, the reader agrees that under no circumstances is the author responsible for any losses, direct or indirect, which are incurred as a result of the use of the information contained within this document, including, but not limited to, errors, omissions, or inaccuracies.

Contents

PART 1: INDOOR GARDENING 1
INTRODUCTION 2
CHAPTER 1: WHY YOU SHOULD START GARDENING
INDOORS 4
CHAPTER 2: THINGS TO CONSIDER FIRST 11
   UNDERSTANDING A PLANTS GROWTH CYCLE 22
CHAPTER 3: DESIGNS FOR SUCCESSFUL INDOOR GARDENS 29
   VERTICAL GARDEN 36
   TERRARIUMS 38
   LIVING ART GARDEN 38
   WINDOWSILL HERB GARDEN 39
   HANGING BASKETS 39
   MATCHING POTS 40
   BALCONY GARDEN 40
CHAPTER 4: SUPPLIES FOR INDOOR GARDENING 42
CHAPTER 5: BUILDING CONTAINER BEDS FOR BEGINNERS 57
   WOODEN PLANTERS 59
   METAL PLANTERS 64
   PLASTIC PLANTERS 66

CHAPTER 6: CHOOSING VEGETABLES FOR INDOOR GARDENS 68

- Carrots 70
- Tomatoes 73
- Squash 76
- Peppers 78
- Beets 80
- Cucumbers 83
- Lettuce 86
- Onions 87
- Spinach 89
- Radishes 92

CHAPTER 7: GROWING HERBS INDOORS 95

- Basil 98
- Cilantro 99
- Chives 100
- Dill 101
- Oregano 102
- Mint 103
- Parsley 104
- Sage 105
- Rosemary 106
- Thyme 107

CHAPTER 8: SELECTING FLOWERS TO GROW INDOORS 109

- Calendula (edible) 110
- African Violet (non-edible) 111
- Chrysanthemums (edible) 112
- Scented Geraniums (non-edible) 112
- Begonia (non-edible) 113
- Hibiscus (edible) 114
- Bromeliad (non-edible) 114
- Chenille (non-edible) 115

CHAPTER 9: FRUIT TREE OPTIONS FOR INDOOR GARDENS 118

- Strawberries 119

- Lemon 120
- Figs 121
- Bananas 122
- Mulberry 123

CHAPTER 10: GETTING STARTED ON YOUR INDOOR GARDEN 125

CHAPTER 11: MAINTAINING YOUR INDOOR GARDEN 130
- Water..130
- Fertilizer 132
- Repotting 133
- Pruning and Harvesting 134
- Pests and Diseases 136

CONCLUSION 140

PART 2: VERTICAL GARDENING.. 141

INTRODUCTION... 142

CHAPTER 1: THE BENEFITS OF VERTICAL GARDENS AND LIVING WALLS 144
- Why are Vertical Gardens Beneficial? 146
- Placing Your New Vertical Garden 147
- Vertical Gardens Are Trendy! 150
- Why Choose a Vertical Garden? 151

CHAPTER 2: WHERE TO PLACE YOUR VERTICAL GARDEN............ 153
- Keeping Your Living Walls Alive 157
- What Type of Plants Should You Choose?..158
- Sunlight vs. Shade 159

CHAPTER 3: PICKING THE RIGHT SOIL 161
- Soil Types 162
- What Nutrients do Plants Need..167
- Adding Nutrients to Your Soil (Organically)................................168
- How Much Soil Do You Need? 169
- Things to Consider When Preparing for a Vertical Garden 170

CHAPTER 4: CONTAINERS, PLANTERS, AND TRELLISES................. 172
- DIYs: Making your Own Containers, Planters, and Trellises......177

CHAPTER 5: THE VERTICAL GARDENING START-UP........................ 182

INSTALLING YOUR FIRST VERTICAL GARDEN 183
DIYing a Drip Irrigation System 188
CHAPTER 6: BEST PLANTS FOR YOUR VERTICAL GARDEN 190
The Best Plants for Living Walls 205
CHAPTER 7: FRUIT TREES FOR YOUR VERTICAL GARDEN 215
CHAPTER 8: VERTICAL VEGGIES 231
CHAPTER 9: GROWING FLOWERS ON A LIVING WALL 244
CHAPTER 10: CONTROLLING WEEDS, DISEASES, AND PESTS 255
Watering Needs 257
Sunlight vs. Shade 258
Imbalanced Soil 258
Pests and Plant Diseases 259
CHAPTER 11: YOUR VERTICAL GARDENING CHECKLIST 263
Steps to Take for Your Vertical Garden or Living Wall 264
CHAPTER 12: FINAL PRECAUTIONS AND CONSIDERATIONS 269
Pros and Cons to Consider 270
CONCLUSION 276
HERE'S ANOTHER BOOK BY DION ROSSER THAT YOU MIGHT LIKE 277
REFERENCES 278

Part 1: Indoor Gardening

How You Can Grow Vegetables, Herbs, Flowers, and Fruits Along with Tips for Beginners Wanting to Build a Container Garden Indoors

Introduction

Indoor gardening is best described as the act of growing plants indoors. It is innovative because it solves many homeowners and apartment dwellers who lack natural space for gardening.

The point of indoor gardening is to create a pseudo gardening environment where you can grow flowers, herbs, vegetables, and even food. Whether you are a gardener seeking fresh produce during winter or someone who has no land to garden on, indoor gardening can be right for you.

This book covers the fundamentals of indoor gardening. From the first to the last chapter, you are offered in-depth information on indoor plants. The first chapter informs you about the compelling reasons you need to build your indoor garden now.

The subsequent chapters explain the types and systems of indoor gardening, the cost of supplies, and the essentials you need before you plant your favorite vegetables, fruits, flowers, and herbs. Then, more information is provided on the best types of indoor plants to have in your indoor gardening and the process involved in caring for and maintaining the garden.

Overall, this book offers comprehensive information on gardening, whether you are a newbie or already familiar with some aspects. By the end of the book, you will be equipped with enough knowledge to start a home garden inside your apartment.

Start reading to unravel the fundamentals of indoor gardening and indoor plants!

Chapter 1: Why You Should Start Gardening Indoors

Gardening is one of the main components of homesteading. Yet, many people avoid it because of the many challenges of starting an outdoor garden. Fortunately, there is the option of growing plants indoors. You can explore this option whether you are a would-be homesteader or an established member of the self-sufficient community.

It is normal to be hesitant about indoor gardening, especially if you are a newbie. Some people are less inclined to try it because they are unaware of the benefits. Plus, they may be afraid to try something new.

But it does not matter once you realize the benefits of indoor gardening. You will be more motivated to give it a chance.

This chapter aims to convince you of the need to start an indoor garden in your home and the benefits of indoor gardening. It will also explain the health benefits of indoor plants. By its end, you should be more excited than ever to start your indoor garden.

There are many reasons why you should consider growing plants inside your home. Everyone has personal reasons to start indoor gardening. Some people start it merely for fun. Others want one because the plants spruce their homes up. However, there are more significant benefits of starting an indoor garden.

Access to fresh produce is one of the most important motivators for indoor gardening. When you have your fruit, vegetable, and herb garden, there is always access to fresh produce. Many gardeners enjoy growing crops indoors because they control the seasons that way.

To have fresh fruits year-round, you only have to plan around the seasons before starting a new crop. There is nothing like "My crops aren't ready for harvest." You can use grow lights, heaters, irrigation, humidifier, etc., whenever you want fruits out of season. These will help provide the right environment for growing fruits.

Herbs are probably the most convenient to grow. You can put them in your kitchen, right next to the window where they can get lots of sunlight, and you can access them for immediate use. What gives a more wonderful feeling than snipping a few chives to mix in with your salad?

A significant benefit of indoor gardening is that it gives you control over the weather. There is no possibility of a violent wind, cold snap, or overly hot weather distressing or killing your plants.

Of course, there are varieties of hardy plants designed to withstand tough climates. But if you plan to grow more tender species, putting them inside your home will improve their chances of thriving and surviving.

Also, growing your plants indoors allows you to customize the whole gardening environment. You can choose how close to the window the plants are, whether they have drafts or supplement natural light with grow lights.

Infestation is another unpredictable element of outdoor gardening, but you can avoid it by establishing your garden inside. Naturally, you might see a couple of mealy bugs, spider mites, scales, and other nasty pests in your indoor garden. But the possibility of an infestation is much lower than when your plants are outside.

The key to avoiding infestation is to thoroughly check for would-be pests and interlopers before bringing new plants home. You can even keep them in quarantine for a few days to ensure they are healthy and safe enough to join your indoor garden. And indoor plants are easier to monitor, meaning you can stop any infestation in its root.

Unlike outdoor plants, indoor plants are protected from mice, rabbits, neighborhood cats, deer, and other animals that enjoy sneaking into outdoor gardens to feast. So, that's an added benefit for indoor gardeners.

Indoor gardening extends your growing season. Even if you enjoy grooming and tending to your plants in open light, growing them inside first provides an advantage. For instance, it allows you to give seedlings and bulbs a head start on the season.

You can start them indoors weeks before the final frost in your region. When it's time to move them outside, simply "toughen them up" by gradually introducing them to outdoor elements. For example, you can place them in a partially shady spot on your patio.

After the regular growing season, you can bring the plants back inside and keep them growing. But remember that moving them back inside the house can shock their systems. So, once again, allow them a transition period in a sheltered spot around your home.

Air purification is another reason why you might be motivated to start an indoor garden. Plants fuel their growth by creating chemical energy through photosynthesis, a process in which water and carbon dioxide convert to glucose.

During the process, they also release oxygen; plants take in carbon dioxide and produce oxygen. That is the opposite of how humans breathe by taking in oxygen and releasing carbon dioxide.

When you grow your plants indoors, this system allows them to act as automatic air purifiers. Many indoor plants can help filter dust, germs, and airborne toxins. Some include spider plants, snake plants, English ivy, and chrysanthemums.

Nothing improves the look of a room more than a bright, blooming flower or a huge, leafy plant. A single plant alone can brighten up any space. Or you can create a brilliant display with your garden to transform the appearance of your living space.

A windowsill of blooming flowers, cactus gardens, or a delicate arrangement of herbs can add a pleasant touch to your home. The environment is just more vibrant when you share your home with living plants.

Another perk of growing plants, herbs, and food inside your home is that you can control your noise exposure. Outdoor gardens leave you with little to no control over the noise of honking cars, barking dogs, loud traffic, or lawnmowers. Loud noises like these can be disruptive and, often, dangerous to your hearing.

An indoor garden is perfect for anyone with tinnitus, a ringing, whistling, or buzzing sensation in the ears. Tinnitus can signify underlying conditions, such as an ear injury, nervous symptom disorders, or hearing loss.

If you use a hearing aid, indoor gardening may suit you better than outdoor gardening. By growing your plants inside, you can get the experience of traditional gardening in a noise-controlled environment. And that can be good for your health.

Gardening is a messy endeavor, mainly due to the use of traditional soil. Luckily, you can grow plants indoors without using soil. Through Hydro Blossom, you can stop worrying about making a mess of your home.

Another type of indoor gardening is *hydroponic gardening*; hydro means water, so hydroponic gardening grows plants through nutrient solutions dissolved in water. Thus, it eliminates the need for soil or dirt. Hydro Blossom is one such nutrient solution. However, the hydroponic method can be complex, particularly for new gardeners.

Additionally, indoor gardens are easier to start than outdoor ones. Sure, you could begin with a fancy and elaborate garden. But the truth is you need not do that unless you have a lot of space to spare.

To begin, you'll need your plants, sufficient sunlight or artificial light, and containers in which to place them. The easiest way to start is to grow herbs on your windowsill. An average herb garden requires at least six hours of sunlight each day.

They are also inexpensive to set up. Your beginning expenses are seeds and plants. You can conveniently skip out on purchasing planters or pots by recycling containers you probably have in your home; butter jars, yogurt cups, and coffee cans are the right size for planting on the windowsills.

Gardening can be a lot of work. As a gardener, you need to tend to your plants, water them, ensure they get enough sunlight, and modify their environment as required. If you have a family, you can use your indoor gardening as an opportunity to teach your kids about responsibility.

By recruiting them to help, they'll get first-hand experience caring for living things and establishing a stable routine. Also, it's a chance to teach them about sustainable living, life cycles, and plant biology. The good thing is that there are varying gardening kits designed especially for kids, making the process even more engaging for your little ones.

Conclusively, plants are good for emotional therapy. Like pets, they make for great company. Tending to an indoor garden goes far beyond that. It's all about caring for another living thing's needs, which can foster a sense of compassion.

You have probably heard that plants respond positively to talking; it's also a form of therapy. Other gardening tasks such as watering, pruning, repotting, etc., are therapeutic when done the right way.

An indoor garden can reduce symptoms of stress and depression because they evoke the feeling of companionship. According to a randomized crossover study by Min-sun Lee, Juyoung Lee, and Yoshifunmi Miyazaki, "interaction with indoor plants may reduce psychological and physiological stress by suppressing autonomic nervous system activity."

This study published in the Journal of Physiological Anthropology suggested that having plants in your immediate living space or office can make you feel calm, comfortable, and soothed.

Medical experts even prescribe gardening to improve wellbeing and mental health. It's also a way of getting exercise, helping you stay fit.

Indoor or outdoor, there are many reasons you should start gardening. It is calming, therapeutic, and enjoyable. In addition, it gives an appearance of natural beauty to your environment. But indoor gardening specifically has some extra benefits that make it even more worthwhile than outdoor gardening.

In the next chapter, we'll consider the fundamental and most important steps to creating your personal indoor garden.

Chapter 2: Things to Consider First

When planning your indoor garden, certain factors determine your success, so give them careful thought. They are things that your plants need to grow, thrive, and survive, which is why you should familiarize yourself with them before you begin.

This chapter will delve deep into these things and why they are important. You'll also learn more about a plant's growth cycle and how these factors influence growth at every stage of development.

Space

Space is the first thing to consider when planning an indoor garden. Yes, the whole point of indoor gardening is to use as little space as possible to create a beautiful green environment within your home. Still, sufficient spacing is at the center of everything. It can make or mar your endeavor.

Like all living things, plants need space to live, thrive, and reproduce. The difference is that they can't move from one place to another like humans and animals. Instead, they need to remain in one limited place to take advantage of available essentials, such as air, water, and light.

This makes them more vulnerable to deprivation. If you don't provide enough space for your plants' growth, you deprive them of essentials. Therefore, you should carefully assess your available space to determine just how ideal it is for indoor gardening.

Think about where to place your garden inside your home. You may think that your windowsill is the ideal location or decide on a sunroom. But some things will determine just how ideal these places are for an indoor grow room.

The thing about indoor gardening is that it can take up as much or as little space as you have available. It depends on how big or expansive you want your grow environment to be. With limited space, you can keep the garden within the shelves and windowsills in your home.

Whether you want a small garden or a big one, your available space determines the kinds of plants you can grow. So, you need to assess and evaluate your home before purchasing certain plants. Still, you can grow all kinds of small or large indoor plants in a tiny space, such as a table or windowsill. If you want a larger garden, you might have to set up a large table or bench.

Shelves make excellent planting areas while taking up very little space. Should you choose to plant on shelves, ensure that you provide the plants with adequate light sources. For example, you might need a grow light to provide supplementary light.

Know your indoor plants' spacing requirements because these change as they grow bigger and taller.

You also need to consider plant spacing itself. Since you will be planting individually in containers and pots, you might think that plant spacing doesn't affect anything. However, separate containers or not, you can't allow your plants to grow too close to one another. If you let that happen, those plants may not receive the required natural or supplementary light. They might even receive less air than they need for proper development, depending on their proximity.

Seedlings and cuttings can be grown near one another, but the spacing requirements will increase as they grow. Eventually, you will need to move them, thin them, or risk them dying off. *(Thinning is achieved by removing the weakest plants to create more growth room for the stronger ones.)*

With sufficient growing space created, the remaining plants can effectively use the available area for their growth. More space means more airflow, which, in turn, means more light for photosynthesis.

As you will soon discover, light and airflow are crucial to plants' growth.

Light

Light is one factor to consider when planning an indoor garden since plants require photosynthesis to survive, which cannot happen without light.

Unless your environment offers sufficient light, your plants can grow tall and gaunt. Even if they produce enough energy for leaves to grow, those leaves might not expand as they should. Insufficient light will hinder the appearance of flowers and fruits.

Light is either natural or artificial. Natural light can be from a windowsill or the skylight, while artificial light comes from grow lights and lamps.

Examine the amount of light, natural and manmade available in your home. Then, consider your window direction.

- North-facing windows receive the least amount of direct light, particularly during the winter months.
- South-facing windows receive the most amount of light. They receive sufficient light from the sun in winter but get less when the sun overheated in the summer months.
- East-facing windows get the best of the morning sun for the majority of the year. They especially receive increased light in cold weather.
- West-facing windows get the best of the afternoon and late-day sunshine.

Remember that your home's lighting condition can shift from season to season. But extraneous elements such as your choice of curtains and window blinds affect it too. It also depends on other external influences such as roof overhangs, shrubs, and trees around your environment.

Before you get any plant, evaluate the hours of natural light the space offers and the quality of that light. Then, go for plants that have matching light requirements with space. Many plants tolerate low light conditions, but that isn't an indication that they are happy.

Suppose your environment doesn't provide the required light level for the kinds of plants you wish to have in your garden. In that case, you can get supplementary light sources to encourage flowering and denser foliage.

- **Low light:** Typically, low light plants are suitable for fairly dark areas, such as a north-facing window. They require very little direct light. These plants hide beneath larger plants' branches in the normal growing environment to avoid direct light. But know that low light conditions aren't appropriate for starting seeds inside the home. Also, plants in low-light environments use less water and mature more slowly. Ensure you don't over-water them in the bid to hasten their growth.

• **Medium-light**: Plants that require medium light are suitable for east-facing windowsills or near west-facing windows. They prefer to be placed in windows that are out of direct light. To start seeds in medium light, you would need additional light sources. Like low-light plants, they don't dry out as easily, so ensure you don't over-water them.

• **High light**: Any plant with high light requirements is best placed in south-facing windows or any other brightly lit location in your home. High-light plants allow you to start seed without using artificial lighting. However, the seeds sometimes need extra light to avoid turning "leggy." Locations with high light make plants dry out faster due to the warmth. So, check your plants more frequently and water them whenever you feel the soil drying up.

In the chapter about indoor gardening supplies, you will discover more about artificial lighting, particularly how to choose the best artificial lights for your plants.

Temperature

Finding the ideal growing temperature is vital for indoor gardening and is one way to ensure bountiful harvests. The atmospheric conditions of an indoor garden can tremendously affect the quantity and quality of finished crops.

Regardless of your skills, you need to make a continuous effort to master all environmental factors that can cause a significant shift in the growth and yield of your plants.

When growers talk about atmospheric conditions, they are referring to temperature and humidity. Some people prefer to lump both together, but they are distinctively different. First, we will explain temperature, then move on to humidity.

Considering the temperature of your grow room is necessary because temperature affects a plant's ability to process light and absorb nutrients and water. It plays a vital role in photosynthesis, seed germination, and fruit/flower development. If a garden's temperature falls below the acceptable range, it becomes less efficient. Then the inefficiencies cumulate and result in lower-quality yields.

Maintaining a consistent temperature in your growing environment is not debatable. The temperature should be uniform from one end of your grow room to another. It should be the same across all areas.

To increase efficiency, determine your garden's ideal temperature range, i.e., the right temperature to maximize plant growth. This is typically crop-dependent since every plant responds to temperature differently. Generally, the ideal temperature range for plants is 65-75°F. It can sometimes vary by 10°F on either side without causing a problem.

A garden consisting of fast-growing annuals should operate at a starting range of 70 to 80°F. Most annuals prefer the higher end of this range, meaning you can use it for both the vegetative and reproductive stages. You will soon discover what both stages entail in the plant growth cycle.

Plants typically prefer warmer environments. If your grow room is cooler, then you might want to stick to vegetables and winter crops; otherwise, you would need to supplement the natural temperature of your home. The closer you get to the optimal growing temperature ranges for the plants in your garden, the better and healthier they will grow.

Plants tend to go dormant in colder months and grow during warmer periods. Still, cool weather crops might not suffer under cooler conditions, while warm weather plants might become diseased and die off.

If you put your garden in a heated room, you might not have to think about additional heating at all. You need only to choose plants that match the average temperature range of the grow room.

For instance, you can grow warm-loving crops like basil in your kitchen since it is typically warm there. Your basement, on the other hand, can be home to cooler plants like parsley.

If the grow room isn't heated, supplementary heat will be needed during a cold climate. The more windows in a room, the higher the temp on sunny days. Supplemental heat is needed on overcast days and nights, which means you will need to install natural gas heating in the grow room or use electric heat.

Before you get your plants, confirm the temperature of your growing environment with a thermometer. Assuming things can get you in trouble.

Note that soil temperature is just as important as the grow room temperature. Growers seldom discuss this since most indoor gardens utilize containers for planting. But it is something worth knowing. Soil temperature is very important to a plant's growth.

Plants, in general, don't like having cold feet. If the garden is cool and the table, shelf, or bench where you sit a plant is cold, the roots can become too cold, and that could cause the plant to struggle.

To fix the problem, you only need a Styrofoam insulation barrier under your growing containers. If the grow room is freezing, the ideal solution is to get a heat map. With hydroponic gardening, you can simply use a water heater to keep the water warm during winter. In the summer months, the growing water can get too warm. In that case, you just need to use a light-colored container for planting or make use of insulation.

Humidity

Earlier, it was mentioned that humidity is the better half of a garden's atmospheric condition. Although it is just as important as temperature, many growers, especially new ones, don't pay mind to humidity. But the good thing is it usually makes itself known.

Humidity is defined as "the amount of water vapor in the air." There is usually a massive change in humidity levels from season to season, and a lack of humidity often poses a challenge to indoor gardeners. Winter is often drier than summer for plants. In winter, you might have fireplaces, furnaces, and heat pumps to keep your home warmer. All of these make the air very dry, reducing the humidity levels in your home. Most plants need humidity higher than growers can offer in the winter months.

How do you know if the humidity in your home is too low for the plants?

- The leaf tips start turning brown
- Plants become withered
- Plants lose their leaves

And sometimes, you might already know about the humidity needed by the plants in your garden, and they are not receiving it.

To increase humidity in your growing environment, use the following tips:

- Give your humidity-needing plants daily spritz to mist them. You can do this with the help of a simple hand mister.

- Increase the proximity of your plants by clustering them together. In their natural growing environment, plants grow in groups. You can recreate this in your home to increase the humidity level. The side benefit is that it also makes the environment look more decorative.

- Place your plants on trays halfway filled with water and some pebbles or rocks. Whenever the moisture evaporates, humidity levels increase. Keep the water halfway up the tray. Don't allow it to reach the tip because this would mean that the pot's bottom has to sit in water. This can cause the roots to rot. Consider slipping a saucer underneath each container. That will help: 1) prevent excess moisture from being absorbed by the plants and 2) prevent the soul from being washed into the tray when you water.

- Purchase a humidifier to use during winter. This can make a huge difference in your garden because the humidifier will help add more moisture to the air, as needed.

- One thing about indoor gardening is that anywhere can serve as a grow room, including your bathroom. Consider placing humidity-loving plants in your bathroom since this part of your home usually has more water vapor in the air. Ferns and air plants are great examples of plants that can do well in the bathroom.

Sometimes, humidity levels can become too high for your plants. High humidity levels for long periods can cause rot. Most of your plants will probably need higher humidity levels, but you must make sure you don't increase it past what they need. Otherwise, you might face problems.

Mold can develop around the plants, including the soil and leaves, when humidity is too high. So, observe your plants for mold, and if you detect none, keep the humidity at whatever level it is.

Remember that it depends on the plants you have. So, research the specific plants you are getting and cater to them according to their individual needs.

These are the four most important things to consider first when planning your very own indoor garden. However, none of these are as important as having the resources.

While indoor gardening isn't as expensive as outdoor gardening, you still need a considerable amount of money to purchase supplies and set up a garden within your home. The chapter about supplies will tell you more about the cost of starting an indoor garden from scratch.

When you talk about resources, you are also talking about time. Indoor gardening is like owning a pet. Your indoor plants demand attention and dedication from you, and you can't offer these unless you make time for it.

Before selecting the plants for your garden, ensure you think about your lifestyle. Only choose plants that require the level of dedication you are prepared to provide. If you lead a very busy life, don't choose plants that demand too much of your time.

Just as you would find a pet that matches your lifestyle, choose plants that fit in with your activity levels.

Understanding a Plants Growth Cycle

As a grower, understanding the stages of growth in plants is crucial for you. Whether you plan to get young or adult plants, familiarizing yourself with the growth cycle will teach you how to achieve maximum yield.

Many growers don't bother with the stages of growth because they think gardening is all about sticking seeds into a container and watering it until a plant appears. However, the needs of your plants change according to each stage. It's best to understand the stages, so you know what needs to meet and when. This is a basic thing every gardener should learn in the planning stage.

Seed

The seed is the origin of any plant. It contains everything a plant needs to survive until the formation of a root. A seed has three fundamental parts: the seed coat, the endosperm, and the embryo.

The seed coat is the outer part of the seed – what you see when you look at it. It is an external source of protection for the upcoming plant.

The endosperm provides everything, including nutrition, that the plant needs in its initial phase. In most seeds, it covers the embryo to serve as a source of accessible sustenance.

The third basic part of a seed is the embryo, containing the roots, cotyledon, and embryonic leaves. All of these things are carefully tucked inside a seed.

Gardener or not, everyone knows what roots are. The cotyledon serves as the external food source once the plant starts to grow. And the embryonic leaves refer to the first two leaves that appear after germination.

Since you will probably buy half-grown plants for your indoor garden, you may not witness the growth cycle at this stage. Still, it's important to be familiar with these concepts and stages; it's what caring gardeners learn.

If you start from the beginning, know that storing your seeds in a dry, airtight part of your home will obstruct them from moving on to the germination phase until the environmental conditions are just right.

Seeds can remain viable for a long time. However, the endosperm declines over time, reducing the possibility of germination.

Germination

Germination occurs when the seed finally emerges out of its shell. Before a seed can germinate, two things must be provided in abundance:

- Water: The growth process is triggered when seeds hydrate and rehydrate regularly and adequately. So, seeds need sufficient water to start germinating.

- Warmth: Heat requirements vary from plant to plant, and heat is crucial for germination. If the environment is too hot or too cold, a seed will stay dormant until the right condition is met.

Germination usually takes days to weeks, depending on what you are planting. Some trees take weeks to germinate, while most vegetables take a few days. However, certain factors can inhibit germination.

First, if you plant your seeds too deeply, they might not be able to come out of their shells. The right thing is to read and follow the instructions that come with your seeds. You shouldn't just use a random amount of soil on the plants.

Some crops prefer to be under the soil's surface, while others need to be on top of the soil. Again, you might not need to worry about this factor if you simply purchase already growing plants.

Second, seeds of poor quality won't germinate as fast as high-quality ones. Make sure the manufacturer you are buying your seeds from regularly tests for germination rates. That will ensure you aren't buying duds. Consider buying from organic and non-GMO distributors. They sell the highest quality seeds.

Third, most seeds prefer moderately moist soil to grow in. If the soil is too dry, the seeds won't sprout. And if there is too much water, the young plant may drown before it can even sprout.

When seeds first germinate, they depend on the endosperm for growth. The seed sends the root deep into the soil to form a support system that can transfer nutrients from the soil to the plant to encourage further growth.

Vegetation

Once the root has established a way for the seedling to absorb nutrients from the soil, the seed still needs to expand its leaves to acquire light and producing the energy it requires for growth.

The vegetative state is when plants grow stem, branch, and leaf areas to access light. The leaves increase and become bigger to create a larger surface area for light absorption.

During this stage, those leaves also need nitrogen for chlorophyll production. Remember that chlorophyll is the material plants need to draw in energy from the light source (s).

Reproduction

This is the phase when the plant redirects energy from growth to flowering. Energy sourced from light is now used to "go to seed." During the reproductive phase, the plant needs phosphorus because it assists with flowering and fruit growth.

You can trigger reproduction by changing the amount of daylight a plant is exposed to daily. Plants have a sensitivity to these changes, which is called photoperiodism. But they only notice the light, not its source.

And that is why you can use artificial lighting to control indoor plants' growth. As long as you provide a measure of light similar to the natural sunlight, your plants will grow indoors.

This stage is also when pollination occurs, which is when plants start developing seeds and reproducing. Since your garden will be an indoor one, you must make pollination happen yourself.

That can be easily done with a cotton swab. You gently brush against a flower's interior and move to the next flower and the next until you have successfully pollinated all your plants. The process is relatively simple and easy, and you don't need it for plants you don't plan on collecting seeds from.

Dormancy

Those who grow perennial plants are familiar with the dormant phase of the growth cycle. Perennials are those plants that live for more than one year. Many gardeners overlook this stage since they mostly grow annual plants, and those do not experience dormancy. But knowing this can be helpful if you plan to grow perennial crops.

In the dormant stage, plants hold off on growth until you provide a more suitable growing environment. It's similar to how some plants hibernate during the summer heat or the winter months. This period can make it seem like your plants are dying off. In reality, they are just conserving energy until an opportunity arises for the life cycle to continue.

Dormancy naturally occurs with seasonal changes due to lower light hours and colder weather during winter. For plants who love the cold, it often occurs during summer. The plants come back right after the heat subsides.

Indoor plants don't experience dormancy as much as outdoor ones, which is another reason to love gardening within the comfort of your home.

Consider withholding a bit of water and fertilizer during the dormant phase because the plants won't absorb as much as they do during other times of the year. On the other hand, suppose your plants start declining when you reduce their water and fertilizer application. In that case, they likely aren't in a dormant phase. So, you should keep treating them normally.

By now, you should have an informed understanding of the growth cycle and the different stages. But there is more critical information to enlighten you on your plants' needs.

Roots

Think of the root as your plants' IV. They take in nutrients, water, and air from the soil and transport these to the leaves to initiate photosynthesis, which is how your plants produce energy for growth.

If you don't create enough space for the roots to grow, the growth of your plant, tree, fruit, or flower is affected. Once the plant reaches a specific size, it may not be able to grow further.

It's like restricting your caloric intake to the number your body needs to maintain its current weight. If you don't add extra calories, you won't be able to add more weight.

But sometimes, your plant might look sickly while seemingly growing great. That might be a sign that your roots require more room to grow and absorb the necessary things to support the plant's development. You would need to re-pot the plant in that case.

On the flip side, you can run into issues concerning too much growth space for the roots. If a container is too big, that leads to "over-potting." The problem of over-potting is caused by too much soil, not the roots.

When you plant in a container larger than what you need, the water you feed the fruit or tree sits in the part of the soil where the smaller root system can't absorb nutrients, water, or air. This decreases aeration, and rather than expand, the roots begin to rot.

This problem only happens with indoor or container gardening since outdoor gardening soil drains water much better.

What happens when your plants' roots become damaged? Fortunately, most plants can regrow their roots after damage. It depends on the extent of damage caused throughout the root system. A plant eventually withers if it does not have sufficient roots to absorb energy (water, air, nutrients).

Leaves

Leaves ensure a plant's growth and continued survival by converting light to energy. To get a little technical, the photosynthesis process produces glucose to fuel the plant. One thing about leaves is that they can communicate with you. Just be a good listener. You can tell your plants' needs from the leaves' colors.

- **Yellow leaves:** If your leaves suddenly start turning yellow, it's a sign that your plants need less water or more nutrients. Stop watering your plants as often as you normally do, but still give them enough water. If the yellow doesn't go away, that could mean they need more plant food due to nutrient deficiency.

- **Yellow spots:** Indoor plants are not completely safe from pests. If your leaves start showing yellowish spots, that could signify a spider mite problem. Scale also occurs indoors, leading to other problems.

- **Brown:** Should your leaves start turning brown and crunchy, it means that your plants need more water. But ensure you don't over-water them. Just give them enough H20 to keep the soil damp. The right consistency of water will ensure that the soil keeps drying up without the leaves turning brown and crunchy.

- **No leaves:** If your plants aren't adding new leaves or the old ones aren't expanding, your plants need more sunlight or water. Without adequate water and sunlight, photosynthesis cannot happen; plants can't add new leaves or grow further. Try giving the plants more water at first. If that doesn't work, increase the light source.

Like humans, plants require certain nutrients that perform various functions, such as triggering photosynthesis or creating a solid root system. The main nutrients plants need are nitrogen, potassium, and phosphorus; every plant needs individual levels of these major nutrients to live and thrive.

Now that you are armed with a more informed understanding of plants and their needs, it's time to put your bright green thumb to work. But first, let's help you choose the best indoor garden design for your home!

Chapter 3: Designs for Successful Indoor Gardens

There are different indoor gardening approaches; each has its own design and style. One by one, we will examine these designs and how you can choose one perfectly suited for your home space and lifestyle.

When talking about indoor gardening systems, people mention vertical gardening, container or pot gardening, terrarium gardening, etc. These are all grouped into two main types of indoor gardening: soil gardening and hydroponic gardening.

Soil gardening is planting with soil, while hydroponic gardening is water-based planting. When you start setting up a green room within your house, the soil is one of the first things you get. You know that plants depend on soil for nutrients and structural stability. The healthier the soil is, the more protected plants are from pests and diseases.

Soil is much more than dirt. It offers oxygen to plants, provides the physical substrate roots need to grow, and contains a diverse community of microorganisms that fuel plants with essential nutrients like nitrogen, phosphorus, and potassium.

Hydroponics might seem like quite a strange method for growing crops to new growers and even old ones. Many lifelong growers stay away from it because it removes everything that every plant needs for growth soil away from the gardening equation.

While soil does provide the listed benefits, the fact is that it is becoming less of a necessity. Modern gardeners consider hydroponics a more convenient way of giving plants what they need from the soil: nutrients.

In hydroponic gardening, plants are grown in water-based nutrient solutions and other kinds of growing mediums without the use of soil. Indoor gardening allows you to plant with soil or hydroponics. If you wish, you can even combine both types of gardening.

Soil planting means growing your crops in containers and pots that you place in different areas across your indoor environment. Hydroponics, on the contrary, has different planting systems. Let's discuss the main hydroponic gardening systems.

- **Deepwater Culture**

This is considered the simplest hydroponics system. What separates each system of hydroponic from one another is the method of connection between plants and nutrients. In other systems, plants are separated from the nutrient solution.

In the deep-water culture system, plants are directly submerged into the nutrients reservoir. The design is simple and straightforward. First, you fill the container levels above halfway with the nutrient solution for the plants.

Then, you place the plants in a polystyrene tray designed specifically for them, which allows the plants to float on top of the water-based solution. As a result, the roots are suspended and constantly wet from the nutrient solution.

There must be an air stone bubbler or an aquarium pump in the tank to prevent root rot due to the never-ending bath. With that, your plants get to soak up nutrients without ever suffocating.

Remember that this system isn't great for all kinds of plants – even with the oxygenated air. However, it is an excellent growing environment for plants like lettuce.

To try hydroponics, the DWC system offers the right introduction, thanks to its simplicity. It is also relatively cheap to set up, making it a great idea if you are gardening on a budget.

The con is that you have to change the nutrient solution faster than any other water-based planting system. Plus, the range of plants you can use with the DWC is pretty limited.

- **Nutrient Film Technique**

This technique is somewhat extreme and complex, but growers who have tried it promise it is effective. The nutrient film technique involves placing your plants in a grow tray, the kind used in a deep-water culture system.

The tray is placed on top of the reservoir tank, which must have been filled with the nutrient solution. It is slightly tilted to place it at an angle. A pump is installed to move the nutrient solution from the tank to the grow tray, flowing over the suspended plant roots.

With the grow tray tilted, gravity makes excess nutrient solution drop back into the tank below. This reduces the amount of nutrient solution flowing over the roots while making it constant. The setup helps prevent overfeeding.

The cycle created by the nutrient pump and gravity makes sure that upkeep is necessary, no matter how small. Another crucial aspect of the NFT system is placing an air pump in the nutrient solution tank to oxygenate the water.

Plants grow faster in the NFT system, likely due to increased oxygenation, and you don't need any medium. Since it is designed to flow constantly, you need not set up a timer like other hydroponic systems.

However, this design is also more expensive than others because of the electricity and nutrient pump cost. Additionally, pumps tend to clog in the NFT system, making it somewhat high-risk.

If you don't check the system regularly and the pump clogs, that could cause your plants to starve off and croak quickly.

- **Wick System**

WICK SYSTEM

Bể trồng với giá thể

Bấc cotton

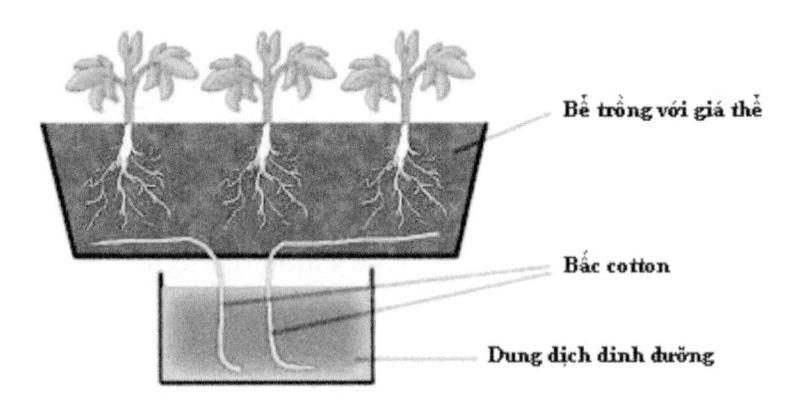

Dung dịch dinh dưỡng

The wick system is as simple as the DWC. It is also easy to set up. In a wick system, you keep your plants in some medium, like vermiculite, which won't take too much of the nutrients. That would defeat the purpose of the medium.

There is no direct contact between the plants and the nutrient solution, which must be in its container. Instead, the plants are fed from the container through a wick. And that is why this is called the wick system.

You can use a cotton or nylon wick. The material doesn't matter, as long as it's absorbent. The best thing about the wick system is that it does not require electricity to run, making it a low-cost choice for gardeners on a budget.

The wick acts as a straw to feed the plants and you, being the grower, only have to check on them occasionally. However, it takes a relatively long time for the nutrients to transport through the wick and feed the plants.

Thus, the wick system is much more suitable for low-maintenance plants, such as herbs. It is not ideal for flowering or fruit-bearing plants due to its limited food availability.

- Ebb & Flow

This is one of the complicated hydroponic systems. The ebb and flow method involves putting plants in perlite, coconut coir, or vermiculite, which serves as a medium. Then arrange them in a large grow tray that goes on top of the nutrient reservoir.

Unlike the NFT, the tray isn't tilted at an angle, so you must drill holes in the bottom to make room for drainage. This system needs a timer to function efficiently. When you set up an ebb and flow system, you must also create a schedule to operate on.

The concept works by having the reservoir pump fill the tray for a fixed amount of time, long enough for the water level to reach the roots in the perlite or whatever medium you use. At that point, the pump shuts off automatically, and the solution trickles back into the tank below.

Setting a timer ensures that the process continues regularly, without underfeeding or overfeeding the plants. This system is best used for plants that have no problem being dry for some period. But you have to set the timer manually. Therefore, nothing stops you from lengthening or shortening the time interval between watering according to the crops' needs.

The only cons of the ebb and flow system are the timer and medium requirements, along with the possibility of the nutrient pump getting clogged. Other than that, it is great for airflow and the recycling of the nutrient mixture. And the timer does all the work for you.

- **Aeroponics**

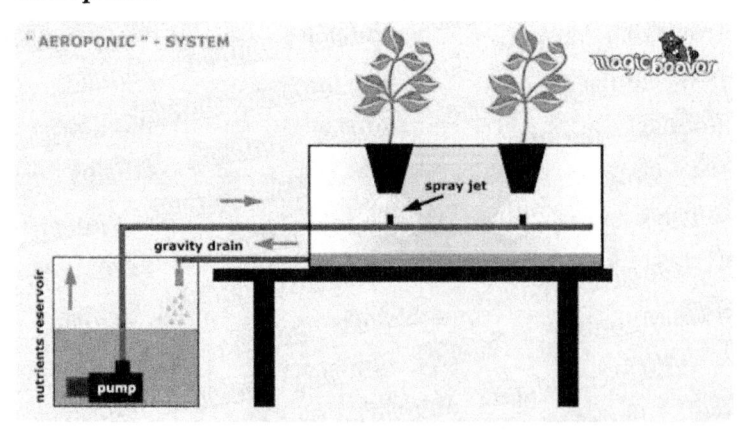

This is the most advanced and most adaptable hydroponic system. Some growers also consider it the "strangest" because of how futuristic it seems. The idea of aeroponics is to hang plants from a grow tray without using a medium, leaving the roots exposed.

Unlike all the other systems, the nutrient solution isn't dripped, transported, sucked, or poured. It's spritzed in the form of a mist. There is a water pressure built within the pump. Then, nozzles spray the solution over the plant's roots like misting your face when waiting in line around a water park.

As you can tell, this is refreshing for the plants. Compared to other systems, aeroponics use less water. Due to this, you must spray the plants as frequently as required, helped by a timer. However, thanks to the need for mist nozzles, this isn't exactly an economical choice because the nozzles are inclined to clogging.

The nutrient solution constantly recycles, and the transformation of water to mist gives the solution higher oxygen levels, leading to faster growth in some crops. Additionally, you get to control the amount and frequency of water sprayed.

These make the aeroponics system ideal for various plants, including vegetables, fruits, flowers, and herbs.

- **Drip Hydroponics**

The drip system is similar to the ebb and flow, but it is much more controlled. The grow tray containing the plants and a medium is placed on top of the nutrient tank. Rather than the medium being flooded, the nutrient solution is deposited at the plants' roots with a drip manifold and drip lines.

Like the ebb and flow technique, this system may be set up with a timer. But this isn't always necessary if the drip manifold contains emitters to regulate the speed of the water. It means you can manipulate the rate at which water gets to every individual plant in one grow tray. That alone makes drip hydroponics a versatile gardening system compared to the other systems.

Suppose you can't decide which to go for between soil and hydroponic gardening. In that case, you can make your indoor garden a blend of both, providing the best of both worlds inside your home.

Soil gardening is mostly done with containers, pots, and built-in planters. The container system is much easier than hydroponics. You can use any material you want, from plastic to metal and ceramic. Some growers even make containers from concrete. A good example is the clay pot.

Chapter eleven will explain more on the process of setting up soil or hydroponic gardening. For now, let's discuss the designs of an indoor garden.

Before you choose a design, you need to consider the space you have available because this will determine the size of your garden. But more importantly, you must consider your aesthetic value and your productivity.

How would you like your home to look when done with your garden? Would you like to make use of every available space in your home or just settle for something simple? Indoor gardening is so convenient that you can even hang plants in your bedroom if you feel like it.

Also, think about how much time you will dedicate towards setting up your grow room and maintaining it. Some garden designs are much more demanding than others. Therefore, choose a design that matches your productivity level. That will help protect your plants from possible neglect.

Different indoor gardening designs can be good for your home. However, suppose you have a small space you wish to maximize to the fullest extent. There, the vertical gardening design is the perfect choice for you.

Below are some of the best designs for a successful indoor garden. These designs take advantage of every potential grow room in a living space.

Vertical Garden

Growing crops vertically is the rave among gardeners right now, and for a good reason. Plants are placed in an upward direction aided by a support system. A vertical garden is one of the most attractive and breathtaking ways to use plants for home décor and gardening simultaneously.

It requires a bit of work to construct and set up. But once you finish, you can turn an entire wall in your home into a stunning display of greenery. Whether you want to fill up your hallway with plants or simply add a dash of nature to empty wall spaces, you can achieve your vertical garden on any desired scale.

Suppose you have little to no gardening space. In that case, indoor vertical gardening can help you utilize areas in your home otherwise unsuitable for growing crops. It is especially great for growing greens and veggies.

You can grow in containers and then place them on walls, fences, patio, balcony, or your porch. Growing vertically opens room for exponential plant growth. It saves space and is healthy for the plants. Simply sitting your containers on the ground makes them prone to pests, rot, and diseases.

A benefit of vertical gardening is that it simplifies harvesting. For example, if you grow fruits vertically, they will simply hang from the vine, making them easier to find and pluck. There are many ways to grow crops vertically.

You can use any of these in your home or combine a few of the designs. You can utilize just about any area for growing crops, and some of the most common vertical systems for climbing plants include:

- Trellises: These are well-known plant support systems. They are used in outdoor gardens and can be used in indoor ones as well. A trellis is generally a flat structure freestanding or attached to a fence, wall, or planter. It comes in different shapes and sizes.

- Pallet container holder: This vertical gardening method can be used for growing herbs, salad greens, and ornamental plants. You just need to arrange a pallet board to hang as many containers or pots as you want. Then, you can place this on your balcony.

- Vertical planter: A vertical planter is used to stack different varieties to make a garden more attractive. You can make one by yourself or purchase it in a local or online store. It is pretty easy to make and can be set up quickly. You only need a minimum of five terracotta pots of different sizes, a variety of plants, potting soil, and a center rod to get started.

Terrariums

Terrarium gardening is achieved by creating plant worlds within a tiny glass environment. Terrariums are mini gardens, and they can be luscious and enchanting. The best thing is that you can put it in any part of your home.

However, the kinds of plants you wish to grow can influence your choice of a garden design. So, ensure you consider what to grow in your terrarium. Decide if a contained glass is the right environment for the crops you want in your garden.

Terrariums rarely have drainage holes, so remember this while choosing the right plants for you. Keep it in mind if you plan to grow plants that don't like sitting in wet soil. But with precision in your watering skills, you can avoid all the problems that accompany the lack of proper drainage in a terrarium.

Living Art Garden

Living art is an enchanting way to display succulent plants. You can get a bunch of pre-made frames just for gardening. Then, all you have to do is fill the frames with plants of your choosing.

Alternatively, consider building your customized living frame with the perfect design, shape, and size. If you are handy with carpentry tools or know someone, try building a deep wooden box.

Then, cover this box with wire screens and attach the picture frame you purchased. Finally, fill the box with soil and peat moss, then put your succulents inside the wireframe. Use various species to create a bright and colorful tapestry of different sizes, textures, and shapes.

Windowsill Herb Garden

The best place for this garden design is your kitchen because that's where it is most functional. Growing a kitchen garden with many of your favorite herbs is a beautiful thing. The mere sight of the varying herbs lining your windowsill is delightful, especially because you know they are only an arm's length away when you need them. With adequate sunlight and window space, you might even be able to grow more than herbs; think tomatoes and chili peppers for your windowsill garden.

A few beautiful pots, containers, or jars are enough to light up the kitchen.

Hanging Baskets

If you don't want plants on your floors and counters, hanging baskets are one of the best ways to display your plants in an indoor garden. They complement an established garden excellently. The presence of nature in your home gives an incredibly refreshing feeling.

Ensure you choose baskets without drainage holes. If they do have holes, consider getting drainage plugs to keep the water from the soil from messing up your floors. You can hang basic planters, macramé hangers, and even glass terrariums. Keep the gardening pots stylish, though.

Matching Pots

Have you ever seen a garden where the grower has all their plants in matching pots? Whether it is terracotta, plain white, or pots with an arrangement of colors, planting in matching pots is a lovely design for an indoor garden.

Select a set of plain or terracotta pots with the same design and varying sizes to create a visually aesthetic theme throughout your grow room. You could try different styles with a uniform color or different colors with a uniform style. Remember to keep the plants in the correct proximity to one another regarding space and light requirements.

This will give your indoor garden a single unifying element and create an elegant display around your home.

Balcony Garden

Suppose you have a balcony in your home; you can grow a variety of vegetables with such little space. Tomatoes, spinach, and lettuce are some of the best crops to grow in pots on your balcony or patio.

Cucumbers, squash, and carrots also thrive well in environments like that. They are considered a new gardener's best friend because of how easy they are to grow anywhere.

You can add several other designs to your indoor garden, but for now, these are the most straightforward ideas to start with.

Below are some tips to help you pick the perfect design for you:

- Stick with the first design you choose. Settling for one design amidst the array of available ones can be quite challenging. And that is why you should pick any design and stick with it. (If you don't, you might never make up your mind!) Consider the exact theme you want before choosing any design, and be sure it fits your home's look.

- Apply the "less is more" concept. You need not grow as many plants as possible just to utilize every available space indoors. That might leave your plants squished and struggling to stay alive. Remember that they need space to breathe.

- Be certain that you have total control over the space where your grow room will be. Avoid spaces where factors you can't control can affect your plants. This will help you gain complete control over the amount of light, air, water, and TLC that your plants get.

Indoor gardens provide you an opportunity to be as stylish as you want with your gardening. It's all up to you to choose the perfect system and design that suit your home and lifestyle as best as possible. Keep everything discussed in this chapter in mind when choosing the right design for your successful garden.

Chapter 4: Supplies for Indoor Gardening

To build a successful indoor garden, you need the right gardening supplies; they make your work easier. Regardless of how small or big you want your grow room to be, you'll want to create a checklist of everything you need.

Before you get supplies, determine the exact kinds of vegetables, fruits, flowers, and herbs you want to grow. This is very important as it will influence your choice of supplies.

Establishing what you'd like to grow and where you'd like to grow them will determine the type of soil, pots, lighting, etc., to purchase. Read to the end to know the recommended plants and make your selection before writing a shopping list.

Also, you need to decide if you will grow your plants from seedlings, cuttings, or adults. Young plants have different needs from full-grown plants. And this can affect the fertilizer and lighting requirements.

You need a handful of specific tools to make your indoor garden a success. Despite what many people think or assume, the tools for indoor and outdoor gardening are quite different. When you think of gardening tools, the first things that come to mind are probably rakes, spades, shovels, cultivators, etc. None of these are meant for indoor gardening.

Gardening supplies can be categorized into essentials and non-essentials. The essentials are supplies you can't do without, needing them to operate and maintain a functional garden. Non-essentials, on the other hand, are supplies that can make your work easier but aren't exactly compulsory to have. You can run a garden fine without the non-essential supplies.

Here are the essential supplies and tools you need to get your indoor garden running.

Pots and Containers

Pots containing potting soil

Once you decide on what to grow, you will know just how much space the roots need. Also, you can determine how big the plants might get. Don't forget that some of the plants you select might need re-potting if the roots become too large for their current containers. Some, in comparison, don't mind staying in smaller pots.

Pots and containers for your plants are some of the basic supplies to get for an indoor garden. Still, you can't just go into your local store to purchase any pot or container you see. Size is vital when selecting pots for your garden.

If a pot is too small, it can stunt your plants' growth. If it's too large, it can obstruct proper drainage and cause your roots to rot. Therefore, you need to know your plants' specific potting needs to find the right-sized pots.

Some other things to consider when buying containers are the material and drainage efficiency. Pots and containers made from upcycled and absorbent materials tend not to hold moisture as efficiently as your roots may need; you'll find yourself watering the plants more frequently. If you are a busy person, this might seem like a hassle and tempt you to neglect your plants.

Plastic and metal containers hold water more efficiently, and they depend on drainage holes to get rid of excess moisture. For new indoor gardeners, drainage holes are important in containers because they serve as a fail-safe for over-watering.

Potting Soil

Unless you want to use a hydroponic gardening system, the soil is one of the basic supplies to get for your indoor garden. But here's the catch: you must get the right type of soil. New gardeners rarely know the difference between topsoil and potting soil. They believe you can use any type of "dirt" for planting.

While topsoil is best for outdoor gardening, it won't drain properly in an enclosed space. Therefore, it is not right for an indoor garden. Potting soil allows for proper drainage since it was made to be fluffier.

If possible, tailor your potting soil according to the specific plant you are growing. Succulents, cactus, and rosemary, for instance, grow well in rough, well-drained soil that contains one-third of sand. Seedlings are best grown in light and soilless mix since that is more moisture-retentive.

A good potting soil consists of perlite, vermiculite, and peat moss. These are soil-less mixes that are moisture-absorbent and compaction-resistant. Still, they are inclined to dry out faster than other potting mixes.

Since they rarely contain nutrients of any kind, you must provide your plants with a regular fertilizer supply. On the other hand, a soil-less mix is great for indoor plants because it is sterile, which means the possibility of introducing pests or diseases is limited.

You might want to add organic matters such as compost peat, leaf mold, finished compost, and garden soil to your indoor potting mix. This is because any growing medium that contains up to 20 percent organic components is less likely to dry out as quickly as a soilless mix. This enables you to add nutrients and beneficial microorganisms to the mix.

When purchasing a potting mix, the most important thing is to ensure that the texture is light enough to make room for water, air, and healthy root growth. Heavier potting mixes are best used for plants that will be in direct contact with sunlight. They won't dry out as fast. Lighter soil mixes are for crops that require little water for root growth.

Some plants need fertilizers once they are in the active stages of the growth cycle. Sometimes, the soil's nutrients become depleted. Other times, the potting mix simply has a low soil ratio. In any of these cases, a fertilizer will come in handy. So, consider adding fertilizer to your shopping list for indoor garden supplies.

You'd need an outdoor garden fertilizer for your indoor plants, so you have to follow the instructions highlighted for indoor plants. You might need to reduce the use to about one-fourth.

Remember that plants in hydroponic gardens rely on liquid nutrient solutions because they need not absorb nutrients from the soil. That means you don't need to purchase soil or fertilizer if you plan to own a water-based garden.

Watering System

Water is essential for plants, and you need to know how much water your garden will be needing; it's imperative for the survival of your crops. Some plants enjoy a downpour of water. Some don't want you to get their leaves wet at all. Some prefer a mild shower, and others just need you to water their bottoms.

You can water your plants with just about anything, but you might want to get watering cans that are designed to mist plants in precise ways. For example, any watering can with an elongated spout gets water below the leaves and directly into the soil. Using a cup, bucket, or jug can cause an overflow of water which can cause root stress.

Plants that enjoy getting a light shower are best watered with a misting bottle or a sprinkler attachment. A drip tray might be essential if your containers have drainage holes. Deep watering means you need larger drip trays.

A larger drip tray is ideal for plants that enjoy bottom watering. Just fill the tray with water and leave the roots to absorb most of it. Bottom watering can also be done with a large container where you can submerge your pot until the root soaks up all the water it needs.

In case you settle for hydroponic gardening, the containment setup will also serve as the watering system. Hydroponic systems naturally come with a water reservoir that must be refilled at intervals, depending on the plants you grow.

Many gardeners like this system combine most of the tools required for gardening into a single efficient gardening system.

Grow Lights

Some houseplants require long hours of direct sunlight season round, while others survive on low light. As you've learned, a south-facing window can provide ample sunlight for the sun-loving plants. However, natural light is not always sufficient for an indoor garden. To grow high-light and medium-light plants with minimal natural light, you must get grow lights.

Grow lights allow you to grow as many varieties of plants as you want without worrying about lighting. You can grow houseplants, vegetables, fruits, flowers, and orchids with a grow light set. They are ideal for starting seeds because they ensure that you get stocky, green seedlings.

You can grow herbs and greens under light with as minimal natural light as possible. But to choose the right light system for your plants, you need to learn how plants use light. Refer to chapter two on how light helps plants.

When purchasing a grow light system, you must consider a few things. Sunlight works perfectly for plant growth because it contains the complete light spectrum and rainbow colors.

So, to grow plants indoors, you need a light system that offers the full spectrum, like the sun. A full-spectrum bulb replicates the natural sun spectrum by producing a blend of cool and warm lights.

This makes them excellent for growing herbs, houseplants, and other crops.

Fluorescent and LED lights both produce full-spectrum light. However, LED lights are much better for the growing environment. Plus, they make less dent in your wallet.

The brightness of a grow light determines the intensity of light received by plants. The plant's closeness to the light source also affects this. Plants' need for light intensity differs according to their species and natural growing environments.

For instance, plants native to sunny climates require more sunlight than plants that evolved in shady forests and tropical jungles. Some houseplants are comfortable being 10 inches away from any light source. If you have foliage plants, they prefer being as far away as possible from a light source. Experts recommend 35 to 36 inches distance.

On the other hand, flowering plants such as orchids, citrus, gardenias, and many vegetable plants need to be as close as possible to the light source. This is because they require a higher intensity for flowering and fruit production.

Another thing to consider with the lighting system is the duration. Regardless of the types of plants in your grow room, they need a rest from light. Plants respire in the dark as part of their growth process.

The duration between active growth time and rest time is key to varying biological processes, such as the fruit and bud setting and the growth rate. Getting a light system with an inbuilt timer enables you to set the preferred duration.

According to their preferred light duration, botanists categorize plants into Short-day plants, Long-day plants, and Day-neutral plants.

Short-day plants need less than 12 hours of daily light to thrive. Before they set buds and flowers, they might even require a series of shorter days. Long-day plants need up to 18 hours of light per day. Most garden flowers and vegetables are long-day plants. They become pale and spindly when they don't get enough light. Day-neutral plants will thrive as long as they receive 8 to 12 hours of light all season.

Grow lights come in different spectrums, sizes, and shapes, so you are sure to find one that fits your budget and plants. There are many cheap lights available if you just need something to give a boost, no matter how little, to your plants.

PH Meter/Soil Test Kit

A PH meter is a necessity in any garden. Whether you are growing with soil or hydroponics, you need it for your nutrient-feeding schedule. You can't afford to feed your plants with nutrients with an unbalanced PH. That mistake can cause nutrient deficiencies and burn. It can also restrict your plants' nutrient uptake.

Of course, you could try measuring the pH of the nutrient yourself. But using a PH test kit or meter can help ensure you never doubt your measurements. It will assist in determining PH levels so you don't end up killing your plants.

Humidifier

It's been established that houseplants need high humidity levels to thrive in an indoor environment. Depending on the area you live in, a humidifier can be an essential supply or not. You can provide your plants with humidity in different ways.

In an earlier chapter, you learned tips that can help increase the humidity in your home for your plants' growth. But consider getting an actual humidifier if these tips aren't enough.

There are three types of humidifiers you can get. They are:

- **Warm mist humidifiers**: These are what most gardeners are familiar with. They work in a straightforward way. You can use them to heat water as high as you want until it becomes water vapor. The vapor is then released to the immediate environment to increase the humidity levels.

- **Evaporative humidifiers:** These are not as common as the former. Unlike warm mist humidifiers, evaporative humidifiers create vapor from airflow. They work like swamp coolers. They draw water from their reservoir through a wicking material which a fan blows air over, thereby adding water vapor to the air. This then flows out into the grow room, providing your plants with the humidity they need.

- **Cold-mist humidifiers:** These utilize less energy. You can also run them for extended periods, making them an ideal choice if you want low maintenance.

You are likely wondering whether the type of mist (cold or warm) your humidifier puts out matters. No, it doesn't. The drop or rise in temperature resulting from the cold or warm mist from the humidifier barely affects anything.

It's up to you to decide if you want a cold-mist or a warm-mist humidifier. The key difference is that warm-mist humidifiers create mist through evaporation, which purifies the water vapor. But they also use a lot of electricity since they heat the water first.

Here's what to look for when purchasing the right humidifier for your indoor plants:

- **Design:** The design of your humidifier should be as simple as possible because you would be using it most of the time. That means it should be easy to take apart and maintain.

- **Run time:** Ideally, the humidifier should have a run time of 12 to 24 hours. You don't want one you have to refill constantly.

Also, make sure the humidifier is small and handy to ensure ease of use.

Hand Fork

Remember that indoor plants have limited access to soil nutrients compared to outdoor plants. Therefore, to keep them healthy, you need to add fertilizer and compost or peat moss to the containers. It's difficult to do this effectively without a hand fork, and that makes it a must-have tool.

A hand fork typically features at least three prongs to help planters work the soil, aerate it, and ensure that nutrients are evenly distributed in the container or pot. You can also use it for planting and transplanting.

Pruners

Pruners are an essential tool no indoor gardener wants to skimp on. You need a well-designed set of pruners to snip stems and leaves. They help manage unwanted growth with precision. However, poor quality pruners can snip off a plant's foliage, which could crush and tear the stems.

That, in turn, leaves the plants vulnerable to infestation and diseases. So, make sure that the blades of your pruners are sharp and of quality. Replace your pruners when the blades start to get blunt.

Keep the blades sharp, clean, and free from disease by wiping them with rubbing alcohol after every use. That will help prevent bluntness and unnecessary damage to your plants.

Plant Sensor

This isn't a necessary tool to have, but it can be incredibly helpful if you don't have much of a green thumb, i.e., you have a plant-killing tendency. It is handy because it lets you know vital facts about your garden and the plants, such as the type, the temperature, and the humidity levels.

The Wi-Fi plant sensor can even send you mobile alerts to check in with the amount of light and temperature that the garden needs and feeding guidelines. If you are familiar with plant care, you don't need the sensor.

But if you've tried your hand at gardening in the past and can't seem to keep your plants alive, then you'll likely find the alerts and guidance from the sensor beneficial. So, if you don't mind spending the money, try to get one.

Neem Oil

Neem oil is an amazing oil for repelling pests and eliminating an infestation. You can add a few drops to the water before misting your plants, or just store it away for whenever you get a bug problem in your garden.

This impressive oil provides you with an organic means of combating plant pests without harming your plants. If you have a pest problem, it will kill the harmful insects and leave the beneficial ones alone. You can use it in an indoor and outdoor garden.

Heat Mats

You already know that your indoor plants require heat to grow. Of course, it's normal for temperatures to plummet during the winter months, but that doesn't mean that your plants shouldn't get the much-needed warmth.

Heat mats help protect your plants against the drastic temperature drop by heating them from below. You just need to place the containers on the heat mat to prevent your plants from getting cold feet and becoming dormant.

Of course, this is also achievable using a grow light beaming down with sufficient heat on the plants. But there's nothing wrong with having both grow lights and heat mats.

Pot Base

Containers for soil-based plants typically have holes at the bottom to encourage drainage and prevent waterlogging. You can collect the drained water and any soil that leaks through the base holes with a pot base.

That means you can easily collect the pot base and get rid of the water whenever you need to. It also means you can reuse it and clean leaked soil more easily. These are ideal for keeping your plants and garden from becoming a dirty mess. After all, you need the display to stay aesthetically appealing.

If you plan to grow a lot of plants, getting multiple packs of pot bases is cheaper. But if you plan to grow a quite heavy indoor plant that can only sit on the floor, it's better to use a rolling caddy that comes with a drip tray.

Rubbing Alcohol/Cotton Swabs

This is one supply that every gardener must have on hand. It is a be-prepared essential for when your plants get a mealybug infestation. Mealybugs look like tiny cotton bits in plants, and you can find them on the root, stem, and leaves.

These cotton-like balls are slow-moving bugs. To get rid of them, simply dip some cotton swabs in rubbing alcohol and dab them directly onto the cotton bits on your plants. That will eliminate the ones visible to you. You can treat the ones you can't see by creating a solution of seven-parts water and one part rubbing alcohol. Put it in a spray bottle and mist your plants with it.

Plant Stands

There is a wide variety of plant stands for indoor gardening. Some are suitable for displaying single plants, while others are designed for collections of plants. You need not go to specialty plant stores to get the best stands.

Look online, and you will find a wide array of sturdy and quality plant stands in different e-commerce stores. Plant stands are ideal if you live in rented accommodation since you can't exactly install shelving systems or hanging hooks around a rented home.

With plant stands, you just need to set them up and start using them. They won't cause holes in the walls, which means no damage is caused to the interiors. That also means you won't have to worry about your landlord sending your deposit back.

Spray Bottle

Not all plants need a heavy downpour of water to grow well. Plenty of them just wants you to mist them occasionally, while others need daily misting. Well, you can't use a watering can for misting. It's much better to get a mister that is dedicated to your plants.

Getting three misters is the ideal thing to do if you really want to be dedicated to your plants. One mister can be for daily water use, another for fertilized water, and the last for chemicals-infused water.

Pebbles or Rocks

Remember we said there should always be drainage holes at the base of plant containers and pots? The problem with this is less about the extra moisture and more about the soil leakages.

One way around this problem is to place a broken clay piece from another pot over the drainage hole to ensure that only water is escaping. If you are extra careful and you don't have any broken plant pots, your alternative is to coat a layer of pebbles around the base of your pots. That will help keep the soil contained.

Another benefit of using pebbles is that they increase the humidity levels as the water evaporates from the holes. That can keep your temperature and humidity at beneficial levels for your plant growth.

Oscillating Fan

Air circulation makes indoor plants perform better. An oscillating fan can help increase the airflow in an indoor garden or grow room. Just ensure you don't use one that directs the air right on the plants. That isn't healthy and can stifle their growth.

That's about all the supplies you need to get your indoor garden running. They will also help with the maintenance.

For aqua and water-based plants, you will need three essential supplies:

- A water tank
- An air pump
- A pipe system

You will also need water-soluble fertilizer. Since that is the only way your plants will get the nutrients they need, ensure you get the highest quality fertilizers. You only need to feed them the nutrient solution once every 4 to 6 weeks when you change the water.

If you live in a hotter climate, you can increase that since some of the water in your hydroponic system may have evaporated. You only need a high-quality water-soluble fertilizer to feed your plants.

Finally, you'll need a water test kit to check the pH levels of your growing water. Ideally, it should be between 7.0 and 7.8, depending on the plants. In general, though, the pH levels should be neutral with neither too much alkaline nor acid.

Additionally, some water test kits can tell you the levels of calcium, chloride, magnesium, and sodium, and inform you of the presence of boron in the water. By purchasing a quality kit, you will learn when to swap the water for a fresh one so there are no harmful or toxic chemicals that can affect your plants' health.

The next chapter delves into something more practical than everything you've learned so far. Discover what it is by reading on!

Chapter 5: Building Container Beds for Beginners

For purchasing containers for your garden, the market is like a buffet. You have an endless selection to pick from. But this only applies if you would rather purchase planters than make them yourselves. If you plan to buy half-grown plants, it doesn't matter since those plants naturally come in containers.

The surest way to fall in love with your indoor garden is to pair the plants with planters that match your style. Now, you can either get these from plant stores or build them yourself. That's your choice to make.

To buy container beds, you just need to look out for a few things the size, drainage holes, and style. These things will also matter if you are building your container beds yourself.

The best thing you can do is make your own planters if regular planters don't meet your specific needs. Or you can recycle materials and objects in your home to make new planters. One thing about **DIY** planters is that they are relatively easy to make. As long as you follow the set of instructions in this chapter, you should have no challenges when building your garden container beds.

Making your planters is also cheaper. So, if you are gardening on a budget, consider building them on your own instead of buying fancy pots and containers from your local or online plant store. That money can be spent on other supplies that are just as important.

Planters can be made from any material or object. You only need to make sure the planter has enough space and good drainage and that the material used is food-safe. The larger a container is, the easier your plants will be to maintain.

A bigger container can hold more soil retain more moisture. In general, you shouldn't build container beds or planters below 12 inches across. Bigger is the better choice for growing vegetables, herbs, and flowers in containers.

Containers are typically made from ceramic, wood, plastic, metal, and fiberglass. Wooden planters can be made from scratch. But to make containers from the other materials, you might have to repurpose objects you already have at home.

Each container bed material has its pros and cons. Let's dive into these so you can decide on which ones you would rather have in your garden.

Wooden Planters

Wood is a great material for building planting pots and containers. You can choose a modern or traditional style and vary the sizes based on the plants you want to grow. Suppose you want a custom-made container that can fit a particular part of your home or match a specific color. In that case, wood is the cheapest and easiest option for you.

With the proper type of wood, the right construction, and adequate maintenance, wooden planting containers can last for several years. Different woods can be used to build planters.

Cedar is a long-lasting wood, but it can be relatively costly. Pine is cheap but may not last as long as you want unless you pressure-treat it with preservation chemicals. Redwood is similar to cedarwood in terms of properties but is more expensive.

Wooden containers are easy to construct because they require easy-to-find materials and tools. If you have storage boxes and wine boxes, you can repurpose them to use as planting containers. The fasteners used for wooden planters should be made of corrosion-resistant metals such as stainless steel.

The disadvantage of wooden containers is that they decay pretty fast if not properly cared for. To prevent rot, always remove the soil from pots you aren't using. Also, ensure you reseal them periodically to prolong the container's shelf life.

Here are tips for building wooden planters:

- If you have some available wooden dresser drawers in your home, those can serve as planting containers. Either separate the drawers for single planting or keep them all in the dresser and draw them out in a graduated sequence to form a beautiful vertical planter.

- Use heavy plastic or nylon materials to line the inside of the containers to last longer. Find plastic bags with bottom holes suitable for proper drainage. Potting soil will go into the bags, after which you can plant the herbs, vegetables, fruits, or flowers.

- Paint the container with bright colors of your choice to add a unifying theme to the garden.

- If you don't have dresser drawers, get wooden crates from a flea market or yard sale. But avoid old painted wood as the paint from those may contain lead, which can be harmful to you and your plants.

- To make the containers sturdier and long-lasting, attach pot feet to keep them elevated. This will make sure they aren't sitting directly on the ground.

- At the end of every growing season, clean out the container and reseal the inside wood. Since you can also plant during winter, just swap the pots for different seasons.

• Don't forget to re-pot when your plants get too big for their containers. Remember that space is key to their survival.

So, how can you build a wooden planter from scratch? Follow the set of instructions below.

Size the Wood

• First, you need to decide on how small or large you want the container to be. This decision should be made based on the number of plants you want in each planter. The size of the area where the planter will sit should also influence the decision. For this example, let's assume you are building a box 6 feet by 3 feet (182.8 by 91.4 cm).

• Purchase your untreated wood, which will work best for the DIY project. You can also use cedar. Both can stay strong against all the possible elements that the planter might be exposed to. For a 6x2 ft. container, consider getting a 14-foot board you can cut down to build the planter sides. Since you intend to use your planter on indoor surfaces such as your deck or patio, you will require one more piece to serve as the planter's base.

• Note: Do not get pressure-treated wood. This contains toxins and chemicals that can kill your plants and add arsenic to your vegetables. A safe alternative to untreated lumber is to use ACQ-treated ones; the process does not include toxic chemicals.

Cut the Wood

• After sizing the wood, you will need to cut it down to the desired sizes. Get a measuring tape to mark out all sides of the planter. Identify the places where you will cut by marking them with a pencil or pen.

• Use a basic hand saw or an electric one to cut the pieces according to size (two 3-foot boards and two 6-foot boards). Be careful to cut as straight as possible.

• If you don't have a saw or you don't want to make the cuts yourself, you can ask the staff where you purchased the lumber to cut it down according to the measurements you want. They may ask you to pay a small fee for this service, but some also cut planks down for free.

Attach the Plank Boards

• Drill pilot holes in the two shorter (3-foot) boards. These will ensure that the wood doesn't splinter when you attach the screws. You need not create pilot holes in the 6-foot planks. Simply drill three holes from the end edge of the shorter boards, with the middle hole in the center of the board width.

• Use galvanized screws or any other kind to fasten the boards tightly. Galvanized screws are recommended because they can withstand certain natural elements without rusting. Line up the boards in a way those with the pilot holes stand on the external corners. Then, use a drill to ensure that every screw goes through the designated hole into the adjoining plank. You may use a screwdriver instead of a drill or drill bit.

• Measure the length and width of the container's inside to ascertain the bottom's size. With whatever measurement you get, cut the bottom plank with your saw. Then, put it inside the box and use the drill and screws to adjoin it to the sides of the planter.

• Next, drill drainage holes in the base of the container. Turn over the wooden box and create at least four holes in the bottom. These holes are important because they protect your roots from getting soggy from excess water in the soil.

Note: If the box is larger than the average planter, add a few extra drainage holes.

Add Finishing Touches

• Line the inside of the planter with a layer of plastic bag or vinyl screen. As noted earlier, the purpose of this is to protect the wood from rot or decay. If you use a vinyl screen, cut it to the same size as the box you used for the container base. Lay it inside and attach it to the bottom with a few small nails. Don't forget to drill drainage holes in the screen parts that line up with the container's drainage holes.

• Smoothen the container by sanding the rough edges. Doing this will help achieve a finished look. Although it isn't compulsory to do, it helps if you will be painting your planters. Use a sander or sandpaper to smooth out the edges and corners. Remove any possible splinters by running the sander along the boards' sides.

• Prime, stain, or paint the planter's exterior. Use paint that matches your home décor or the theme you have in mind for your indoor garden. You can also stain the box to allow the wood's colors to shine through. If the box is made from cedar, you can leave it alone without painting or staining, as the wood is a beauty in itself.

Note: Do not treat the interior of your planters as the treatment may contaminate the potting soil, and as a result, your plants. Instead, line the box with holes-laden plastic or nylon to protect the lumber.

After you have created the wooden container box, you can add a thin gravel layer. Then, add the potting soil for planting. The gravel is there to help drain the box when necessary. Remember that the soil or compost used is determined by the types of vegetables, flowers, fruits, or herbs you intend to grow in the container bed.

There, you have a new wooden planting container in which to start growing your favorite indoor plants. As you can see, DIY wooden planters are easy and straightforward to construct.

Metal Planters

Metal containers can make an indoor garden look fabulous. From tin cans to modern steel boxes and feed troughs, you can achieve a wide range of looks and styles with metal planters. A file cabinet can be repurposed to become a container bed. Whether shiny, painted, or brushed, all kinds of metal surfaces can work for metal planting containers.

Many gardeners consider metals an unusual choice of planting material. Still, they can add a unique look to your indoor garden. Plus, they are great as accent pieces. Look in your home, and you will find many old metal objects waiting to be reused as metal planters.

Perhaps the best thing about metal planting containers is that they develop attractive worn patinas when you leave them in the weather. For example, a copper pot may add an attractive touch of green over time. That improves the attractiveness of the planter and your garden.

Although they will end up rusty or corroded, metal planters can last for several years before they give in to corrosion.

The one disadvantage is that metals tend to get hot during the summer months or generally under hotter temperatures. If you aren't careful, this can make your plants burn and dry out the moisture in your planting soil quite quickly.

Fortunately, indoor gardening offers a way around that. You can use metal containers in the shadiest locations. Use them for low-light plants since those require minimal direct contact with the sunlight.

Tips for using metal containers as planters:

- You can use metal items as cachepots by setting a fiber or plastic container inside the metal container.

• Create drainage holes in the bottom of the container with a can opener. Or you can pound the holes in with the help of a large nail or an awl. The more holes you put, the better.

• Find plant colanders, metal cans, old BBQ grills, and other cheap metal containers that can be used for growing single plants.

• Don't forget to line the metal container itself with plastic material. Ensure you cut some drainage holes into the plastic as well.

Plastic Planters

Plastic is a diverse material for making planting containers. Some plastics are high-end and attractive, while others are cheap and bare-looking. But it doesn't matter whether you decide on a quality decorative foam container or repurpose a pail you once used to keep things plastic planters are practical.

For gardeners on a budget, plastic containers make a perfect choice because they are the least costly material. They are also lightweight, so you don't have to worry about heavy lifting. Additionally, plastic is the most diverse material, meaning you have hundreds of styles and options to choose from when buying or repurposing your planting containers.

A disadvantage of growing with plastic containers is that some can leach toxic chemicals into your soil, especially if you leave them in direct contact with the sun. Before you buy or repurpose any plastic for growing your edibles, make sure it is food-safe.

Tips for creating plastic pots and containers:

• Find old plastic pots you no longer need and spray them with enamel to give them a brand-new look.

- Use old plastic pots as liners for metal and terracotta planters.

- Apply plastic polish on faded plastic pots to restore the shine and gloss.

You have a limitless range of options to choose from when making DIY planters and container beds. It all depends on how imaginative and creative you are. Don't underestimate the usefulness of ordinary objects around your house.

Many, from teacups to whiskey barrels, can all serve as containers for your plants. Ensure you make drainage holes in any material you use for your container bed and that the potting soil is mixed appropriately.

Remember that the smaller your container, the less soil mixture you can put it. Therefore, the soil moisture level must remain correct as you have little room for error.

Find beautiful images of wooden, metal, plastic, and other planters made from random objects around the house and make your pick.

Chapter 6: Choosing Vegetables for Indoor Gardens

There are different varieties and options to choose from when selecting vegetables for your indoor garden. Most vegetables are warm-season crops, so they are harder to grow during colder months. Winter leaves outdoor gardeners wishing they had fresh produce from the summer.

But when you have an indoor garden, you won't have to worry about not having fresh veggies and greens for your consumption. The good thing is that the process of growing vegetables indoors is more straightforward than you think.

No matter your reason for starting an indoor vegetable garden, you want to ensure that you have the best gardening experience. The only way you can do that is to choose vegetables proven to be suitable for indoor gardening.

Vegetable gardening shouldn't be a difficult task if you care for the plants the right way. Before you choose a specific crop, learn about the growing requirements. As long as you create the right environmental and growing conditions, you will have a bountiful garden filled with delectable home-grown veggies in little time.

The thing is, you can grow most vegetable varieties indoors as long as you meet the growing requirements. That is the only thing that could pose a challenge.

This chapter will detail the ten vegetables you can grow indoors – both their growing requirements and growing process. More examples of veggies suitable for an indoor environment will also be provided.

Before we get to it, know there are two main varieties of crops: heirloom and hybrid. The key difference is that you can save heirloom seeds from your veggies for the next planting season, but you can't do that with hybrid seeds. Heirloom crops pass on the exact features of each specific cultivar from season to season. So, if you save seeds from a plant this season, the seedling will have the same growth habit, size, flavor, and color in the following one.

Conversely, hybrids don't retain the characteristics of a parent plant because they comprise two or more cultivars. Therefore, the traits are typically mixed up.

Heirlooms tend to have superior size, color, flavor, and growth, which is why they are recommended for an indoor garden. To grow heirlooms, know that you can't save seeds from hybrid crops as those won't give you the same plant as the parent.

However, suppose you don't have plans of saving seeds from your harvest for the upcoming seasons. In that case, you can grow hybrid vegetables in your garden. Just make sure you grow them according to instructions.

Tomatoes, peppers, lettuces, peas, eggplants, beans, and other self-pollinators are some vegetables that can be used to save heirloom seeds because they replicate the same qualities as parent plants. To prevent cross-pollination and avoid having hybrids, you need to plant insect-pollinated heirloom veggies several feet away from one another.

So, what are the ten best vegetables to grow in your indoor garden? Check them out below.

Carrots

Carrots are reputably difficult to grow, especially in an outdoor garden. But most gardeners find them relatively easy to grow in containers. With the right conditions, you will love the result of your container vegetables.

Some varieties of carrots are best grown in fairly-sized containers. Still, if your planter is big enough, you can try growing some of the larger varieties. Just know that smaller types give you a much quicker harvest, and they are generally more fun to grow.

Containers are ideal for growing carrots because of potting soil's loose and loamy nature, which, as you already know, is what you use for indoor and container gardening. That kind of soil gives the carrots room to stretch out.

Radish-shaped carrots don't take up much container space, so consider growing these varieties. Still, there are others you can experiment with to see which one works better with your hands. Some include:

> • Romeo is a fast-growing variety that is small and well-fitting for a container. It is round and about two diameter inches.

> • Paris Market a small, round French variety you can harvest in 50-65 days. They are sweetest when they are no bigger than two diameter inches.
>
> • Nantes are typically ready to harvest in a 75 days max. This variety is long but shouldn't be allowed to go beyond 7 inches before harvest. The ideal growing temperature is between 45°F and 75°F. It is great for new indoor gardeners.

Other carrot varieties to consider growing are Thumbelina, Danvers, Imperator, and Chantenay.

In an indoor garden, your carrots should be in a location where they can receive up to six hours of natural sunlight every day. Even when cloudy, they will benefit from any amount of sunlight they get.

Carrots do well in loose soil with enough room for drainage, so don't make the potting soil mixture hard. Get rid of all possible obstructions such as rocks, pebbles, gravels, glass, or any other thing that can cause your veggie to become stunted or deformed. The potting soil should be of the highest quality.

Consider purchasing potting soil made specifically for vegetables as they contain all the necessary nutrients and requirements. Plant your carrots a few weeks before the final frost. Although they are cool-season crops, young carrots don't do well in extreme frost. So, keep the temperature at the right level.

You can grow carrots in any container that is not less than 12 inches wide and deep. The deeper, the better because carrots need plenty of space for healthy growth.

Tips for planting carrots in containers:

> • Fill your planting container with potting soil to around 3-4 inches from the top.
>
> • Sprinkle the seeds all over the soil surface, then add more soil to cover.

- Water every three days to keep the soil moist. Do not let the soil dry out, but also avoid letting water sit in the planter.

Germination can take up to three weeks, so don't be in a hurry to see carrot leaves sprouting. When the seeds germinate, you will need to thin them to provide more space for your carrots. Get rid of the weaker and smaller ones to give space for the remaining carrots. There should be at least two inches of space around each carrot in your container.

Once you have the baby carrots, continue taking care of them until they start to pop out of the soil. To care for them, you need water and fertilizer. Feed them with a balanced organic foliar fertilizer every three weeks. Don't use too much manure or nitrogen-laden fertilizers because those can cause your carrots to deform.

Water according to the soil and environmental conditions. As noted, you should keep the soil moist enough without soaking. Soil dries out faster in containers, so stay on top of your soil condition.

Suppose you live in a dry climate. In that case, try using a self-watering container to plant your carrots. That will help keep the soil moist and healthy.

Carrots can be planted in companionship with these plants:

- Cherry tomato
- Lettuce
- Radish
- Chives
- Sage
- Rosemary

Don't plant them around potatoes, parsnip, and dill.

Tomatoes

Homegrown tomatoes are probably the best things ever. If you know someone with a passive dislike for tomatoes, all it takes is one homegrown tomato to make them change their tune. Nothing tastes as juicy as a red, ripe tomato fresh out of a garden.

Not only do tomatoes taste great, but they are quite straightforward to grow. Except for extreme frosting temperature, you can grow tomatoes in almost any condition. They don't require plenty of space, which makes them perfect for indoor gardening.

You also have various varieties to choose from, depending on your personal preferences and region's hardiness. Cherry, Roma, Beefsteak, Long Keepers, and Main Crop are some of the most common tomato varieties to select from.

- Cherry tomatoes are probably the easiest type to grow. They mature early, and children love them. They can be grown in any kind of indoor planter.

- Main Crop tomatoes are the most commonly grown variety in many home gardens. They produce a bountiful harvest during mid-season.

• Roma tomatoes are also called *plum tomatoes*. They are small and long and are generally grown for canning.

• The Beefsteak is a large variety of tomatoes, which is why it is called the "big daddy of tomatoes." It is great for sandwich making. However, it never really matures until the growing season is well underway.

Most orange and yellow tomatoes are called Long Keepers because they can be stored for many months in cool and dark areas.

Tomatoes follow two growth patterns: Determinate and Indeterminate. Determinate growth means that the plant will grow to a specified height and width, flower, and spend the rest of its time ripening. Varieties that follow the determinate growth pattern are the best options to grow in a planting container or pot.

Conversely, indeterminate growth means that the plant will keep growing all season until the frost comes, which is when it dies. Varieties that grow indeterminately never stop adding width and height, so they aren't ideal for indoor gardens.

The growing time should determine the tomato variety you grow. Some take as short as 50 days, while others like beefsteak take up to 90 days to produce fruits.

If you want tomatoes you can use for a sandwich, go for the beefsteak variety. Looking to make salsa or sauce? Use cherry or Roma tomato. Note that cherry isn't suitable for sandwiches.

Tips for planting tomatoes:

• Put the planter in a location where your tomatoes can receive over six hours of pure sunlight and up to eight hours of light in general.

• Make sure the soil is loamy and well-draining with a pH level of 6.0 to 6.8.

- Start seeds every two to three weeks to grow tomatoes all season round.
- The ideal indoor temperature for tomatoes is 65°F or more.
- Use 6-inch containers and plant them ¼ inches deep.

In the beginning, keep the growing pot in a warm location, such as the top of your refrigerator. Germination should occur in 5 to 10 days, after which you can move the container to a more brightly lit location, such as the south-facing window.

The warmer the temperature, the quicker the plant will flower. Warm temperature also promotes growth. Once the seedlings are at least 3 inches big, move them to a bigger container. Then, start fertilizing bi-monthly.

Some of the smaller varieties suitable for growing indoors include:

- Tiny Tim
- Red Robin
- Florida Petite
- Toy Boy

Consider the fruit type, size, growth rate, requirement, and ability to set fruit in a cooler climate before choosing any variety of tomatoes. Many gardeners find that Red Robin has the perfect characteristics for an indoor environment.

Squash

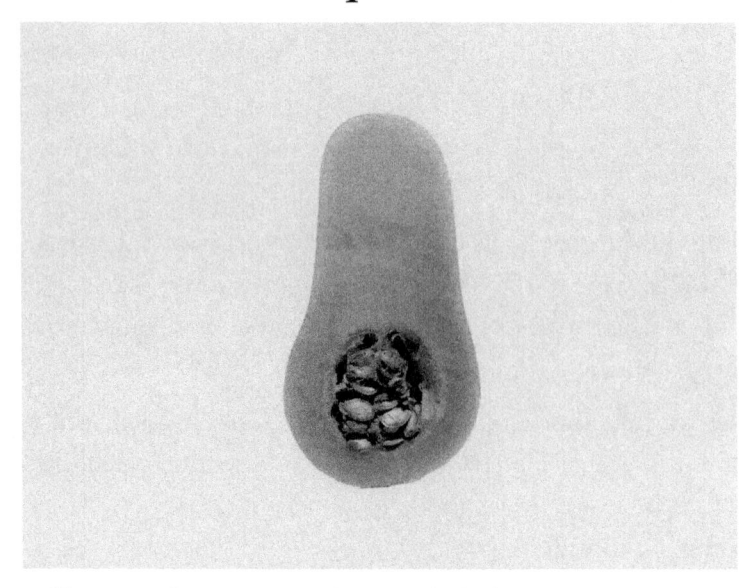

If you like squash, you may be worried that you can't grow them inside due to their large tendencies. Fortunately, there are varieties of squash perfect for indoor growing, so you don't have to fret about missing out on fresh squash supplies.

Several varieties of squash can be grown indoors. They are categorized into summer and winter crops. Most are vine plants, but there are a few bush varieties as well.

Summer varieties are large and bushy. They don't spread as vine squashes do. Some of the most common types are:

- Scallop
- Straight-neck
- Crooked-neck
- Zucchini

Winter squash varieties are vine plants, which means they will spread throughout your garden. They are categorized according to sizes, colors, and shapes. Some of the most common ones are:

- Acorn
- Spaghetti
- Hubbard
- Butternut

The summer varieties are the best to grow indoors because they require less room for growth, making them suitable for container gardening. Still, they give the same amount of harvest as those you grow in outdoor gardens.

Like any vine-growing crop, squash prefers warm temperature. Yet, they are hardier than cucumbers and melons. They need full sun, adequate moisture, and a fertile potting mix to grow and mature well. You should add sufficient composted materials into your soil when making the potting mix.

Both summer and winter squash are best grown in well-drained soil with high organic matter content. Add peat moss or compost into the soil to get the desired level of organic matter.

If you plant your squash seeds in a container around early July, it should take only 50 to 60 days before you have fresh squash to harvest.

Tips for growing squash in an indoor garden:

- Place a piece of fiberglass screen at the bottom of your planter. Ensure it covers the drainage holes to keep pests out and keep the soil in.
- Fill the planter with your potting mix until it's about 2 inches from the top.
- Put the squash seeds in the center of the container and add ½ inch of the potting mix to cover up.
- Water the soil until the drainage holes release excess water. Put the container in a location where your squash can get up to 8 hours of daily sunlight.

• Ten days after planting, when the squash germinates, thin the plants by cutting the weakest and smallest seedlings with scissors. Leave the two biggest seedlings.

• When the seedlings are 8 to 10 inches tall, cut the smaller of the remaining squash plants from the soil line.

• Fertilize your squash when it is around two weeks old. Then, wait until a week to harvest before you fertilize again.

• Water the plants any time the top layer of the soil feels dry. Regularly check for signs of pests or diseases.

To mix your potting soil for squash, use equal parts of compost, perlite, and sphagnum peat moss. Before mixing with the compost and perlite, moisten the peat moss to allow for easy combination.

Peppers

If you are looking to add bright colors to your garden, peppers make a great addition. From red to yellow, orange, green, and even purple, peppers have various colors that make them ideal for creating a colorful indoor garden. They come in varieties, from sweet to hot and spicy. Peppers are easy to grow, but temperature often poses the biggest challenge for many gardeners. It is probably the most important factor when growing peppers indoors.

Bell peppers are one of the most common varieties of peppers. You can produce regular bell pepper for your consumption with the right nutrients and growing environment. Below are tips for growing some inside your home:

- Mix coarse sand, vermiculite, and peat moss in equal parts to create your potting soil. For each container, make two gallons of potting mix. Add in two spoons of fertilizer with phosphorus, potassium, and nitrogen in a 10-10-10 ratio.

- Cut cloth in the shape of a circle. Make sure it is many inches longer than the bottom of your container. Place the cloth at the base and press the edges against the planter's sides.

- Pour your potting mix into the cloth until it is about one inch away from the top.

- Drop two seeds into the soil nearest to the center of the container with at least 3 inches gap between both. Use your finger to push the seeds deep into the soil until a thin soil layer submerges them.

- Dampen the soil with water, but be careful not to over-saturate it. Put the container in a location where the pepper seeds can receive natural sunlight throughout the whole day.

- Keep the temperature in the grow room between 65 and 75 degrees. Make this consistent.

• Water the soil regularly to prevent it from drying out. Once the seeds start flowering, use a water-soluble fertilizer to fertilize them every week. Again, the nitrogen, phosphorus, and potassium ratio should be 10-10-10.

• Look out for peppers to form. Wait until the peppers develop a sharp red hue over the entire surface before you harvest them.

Beets

Beets are the easiest vegetables to grow during the winter months, making them right for indoor gardening. As long as you keep the soil temperature above 40 degrees, you can supply your home with fresh beets year-round.

Naturally, beets have different varieties, from dark red and striped beets to sugar ones. No matter which ones you want to grow, a container is good enough to grow them indoors. Still, some varieties are much more adapted to indoor growing than others.

Some of the best beet varieties to grow indoors are:

• Cylindra has the shape of a carrot, contrary to the usual round look most beets have. This is an heirloom variety and is sometimes called the "butter slicer" or the "Formanova." It takes just 60 days to grow and harvest. The Cylindra is a unique variety because it's cylinder-shaped, and that's where it got its name.

• Detroit Dark Red makes a colorful addition to any garden. By now, you should know the aesthetic and nutritional importance of adding a dash of color to your garden. If you don't know, the more colors you have, the more natural vitamins you will get from your plants. The Detroit dark red variety is a versatile beet type you can grow in varying temperatures and soil conditions. It also takes just 59 days to harvest.

• Chioggia is typically ready for harvest in 55 days. It is an Italian heirloom variety with an incredible flavor. It will make a great inclusion in your garden.

• Golden gets its name from its natural golden color, which differentiates it from other beet varieties. It can be grown and harvested within 55 days.

Other varieties include Mangold, Lutz Green Leaf, and Sugar Beets.

Tips for growing and caring for any variety of beets:

• First, beets are cold-weather crops. Therefore, they need a consistent soil temperature of 40°F. If the temperature is too hot, germination won't happen. If you live in a colder climate, you can plant beets all winter long. You can also plant it in the summer if you adjust your environment to match the growing requirements.

• Beets need loose, loamy, and well-draining soil to grow well. They also need part sun. The soil pH level should be between 6.0 and 7.0. Ensure there is sufficient compost in your potting mix before you plant beets.

• You can also use clay soil, but make sure you mix in lots of sand to improve the soil's texture and drainage.

• The first fourteen days after planting your beets, water them every day. Once the seeds start germinating, you only need to water the crop every 10 or 14 days. Insufficient watering can cause serious problems for your beets, so pay attention to the moisture level.

• Once the plants start sprouting, thin them out the same way you would your carrots. Keep the space between your beets 4 inches apart. Overcrowding can severely damage your harvest.

Cucumbers

Basically, there are two types of cucumbers, and both types come in different varieties. The first is the slicing cucumber, usually about 15 to 20 cm long, while the second is the pickling type. This one is shorter and never goes beyond 3 to 4 inches once fully mature.

Some cucumber varieties were bred to fruit even in an enclosed space since cross-pollination can't happen. Therefore, they are the best to grow in your indoor garden. Before you start planting cucumbers, though, there are some things to consider.

Forget about buying garden variety seeds because those won't grow well inside your home. Instead, settle for non-genetically modified (GMO) seeds because their seeds are more likely to germinate in an indoor garden.

Non-GMO seeds usually require more work in terms of pollination and pest/disease prevention. They also tend to produce fewer cucumbers compared to the seeds suitable for outdoor gardening. So, be sure you purchase seeds bred for indoor gardening.

The varieties of cucumbers for this purpose have flowers that pollinate themselves. They are disease-resistant and generally give a higher yield.

Bush cucumbers are varieties suitable for planting containers, as well as outdoor gardens. Some of the best ones include Bush Champion, Patio Pickler, and Bush Whopper.

Like squash, cucumbers are vine plants, so they need lots of space to grow well. If you are using a container, you need a big one to accommodate the large cucumber leaves. Otherwise, they will grow out of control.

Also, it's best to plant them with a vertical support structure such as a trellis to tell a major amount of the weight. Cucumbers like to sprawl and trail as they start growing. The tendrils are fast-growing, and they attach to anything within reach. So, be sure to pick a location with a lot of space.

Cucumbers need at least six hours of sunlight every day for optimal growth. Even then, you need sufficient light from additional grow lights if you want them to mature quickly. Without adequate sunlight, the cucumber plant's growth might be slow. This could lead limit your yield and cause the plant to produce smaller fruits.

You can purchase cucumber seeds the first time and then start saving seeds for the subsequent seasons from your previous plants.

Cucumbers grow well under a humid temperature, with loose, loamy soil and, as you've learned, plenty of sunlight and artificial light. The soil should have compost and fertilizer to give your cucumber plant the much-needed nutrients.

Before planting, get rid of all sticks, rocks, and debris from the soil. Then, mix enough organic matter and fertilizer into the potting mix.

Note that most cucumbers need a female and male flower to pollinate. The ones that don't are parthenocarpic, which means they can flower or set fruit without pollination. A good parthenocarpic variety that can be grown indoors is the Arkansas Little Leaf.

As the gardener, you can grow your cucumbers hydroponically or in soil. Most prefer to grow in water, however.

Tips for planting cucumbers indoors:

- Make your potting mix with equal part soil, compost, peat moss, and perlite, specific to the cucumber needs.

- Use a large ceramic or plastic container 12 inches wide and 8 inches deep, with plenty of drainage holes to get rid of excess water. As much as cucumbers like lots of water, they also like good drainage.

- Plant them around 2.5 cm deep. Once the plants start sprouting, think of the smallest and weakest ones as needed.

- Put your container in a location where the cucumbers can climb on a trellis or any other vertical support structure. That will lift the fruit off the soil and reduce the amount of space needed.

Following the tips above will ensure your garden has a neat appearance. Don't forget that the bush and compact varieties are the most suitable for growing containers and pots in enclosed spaces.

Lettuce

Lettuce is one vegetable you must have in your garden. It is a cheap way of keeping salad greens on your table. Lettuce is a cool-season veggie, so it grows better in a moist environment. This makes it perfect for a hydroponic system. But this doesn't mean that you can't plant it in soil.

Most lettuce varieties are better grown in cool conditions. Even if you live in a colder climate, you won't need to worry about the frost because the seedlings can tolerate it to an extent. Lettuces actually grow better at a temperature of 45 to 65°F.

For you to understand your lettuce's taste and flavor, they need to grow very quickly. So, before planting, you must have mixed the soil with organic compost and high-quality fertilizer to encourage rapid growth. The soil pH should be between 6.2 and 6.8.

Tips for growing lettuce indoors:

• Due to the seed's small size, sprinkle it on well-mixed soil in a plastic or wooden container. Then, lightly cover with a small layer of soil.

• Don't plant too deeply because the seeds require adequate sunlight to emerge from the soil.

• Mist the pot gently with the spray bottle to avoid displacing the newly planted seed with water.

• For optimal growth, give your lettuce up to 2 inches of water every week.

• Place the container around taller crops like tomatoes so they can provide the shade the lettuce needs. This will also help conserve space in an indoor garden.

Onions

Imagine having an indoor vegetable garden without onions. That's impossible, right? Onions are some of the best vegetables to cook with. You can use them on salads, and they add variety to different meals. Overall, they are just amazing.

So, you definitely should have some in your indoor garden. The great news is that onions are also eligible for your container gardening project.

Growing onions in containers is the same as growing them in the ground. The only difference is choosing the right container, depending on the number of onions you want. To get a decent yield, you need to plant several onions.

Therefore, attempting to grow them in smaller pots about 5 to 6 inches wide may be cumbersome for you. It is better to plant your onions in a wide-mouthed container at least 10 to 12 inches deep. It should also be several feet wide so you can have enough space to grow many onions that would be worth your time. Onions are also growable in tubs and buckets.

Regardless of the type of container you want to grow your onions in, location is the most important thing. Your onions should be in a part of the house where they can get up to seven hours of light per day. If you don't have an ideal location like that, ensure you supplement the natural sunlight with grow lights.

Water is key to onion growth, especially in a container and enclosed space. Onions need at least 3 inches of water every week. They might need more in hotter climates. Check them daily, and add some water whenever you notice that the topsoil is drying out.

If you plan to use a tub to grow your onions, the best part of your house to put that is the patio. That is where you can have the most fun by trying your hands at different varieties of onions.

Note that the more leaves you see at the top of the plant, the more inside the onion layers. What that means for you is that you have some big onions to harvest during harvesting time.

Some of the best varieties of onions to grow in an indoor garden are:

- Yellow Cipollini
- Ailsa Craig

- Red Baron
- Evergreen Bunching
- Valencia
- New York Early
- Walla Walla
- Gladstone

Best plants to surround onions with:

- Tomato
- Lettuce
- Chamomile
- Strawberry
- Rose

Don't surround your onions with beans, safe, garlic, peas, asparagus, leek, etc.

Spinach

Spinach is the perfect addition to your vegetable garden if you eat healthily and are gardening on a budget. You just need some affordable seeds, light, and a tiny space to start growing spinach.

In the past, it used to be known as the slimy, unattractive veggie that no kid likes. Nowadays, though, most of us know how delicious this green can be. Getting started with growing spinach is easy.

First, there are three major varieties: savoy, smooth, and semi-savoy. The smooth variety is sometimes called flat spinach. Newer varieties of spinach are constantly being developed to increase the growing season and improve the taste and flavor.

Savoy spinach is a sturdy variety with wrinkled and crinkled leaves all around. It has great cold tolerance. As you might have guessed, this variety is much harder to clean after harvest. Rather than wash yours under water, you are better off soaking them in cold water.

Hammerhead and Bloomsdale are the two most commonly known savoy spinaches. The former takes just 27 days to mature, while the latter takes 30 days. Hammerhead is mildew-resistant, and Bloomsdale has a knack for bolting rapidly.

Semi-savoy spinach is another cold-resistant, sturdy variety, but those are not its most notable features. It is more known for being disease-resistant and bolt-resistant compared to its savoy counterpart.

Semi-savoy is less wrinkled than savoy, which means cleaning the leaves is easier. However, the seeds mature a little slower than savoy seeds. Reflect, Tasman, Kolibri, Acadia, and Tundra are some of the most common semi-savoy varieties to plant in your indoor grow room.

The third main variety of spinach is the flat-leaf, similar to those you find in your local grocery. There are no crinkles and wrinkles on the left, so the leaves are easy to clean. This variety is also bolt-resistant.

Lizard, Seaside, Red Kitten, Woodpecker, and Flamingo are some of the most common flat-leaf spinach varieties. There are also some heat-resistant varieties, such as Malabar and New Zealand.

Compared to most vegetables, spinach offers a positively easy gardening experience.

Tips for growing spinach in a planting container inside your home:

- Use a container or pot 6 to 7 inches deep.

- Spinach needs full or partial sun, so place the pot in a windowsill location where it can get up to 5 hours of sunlight per day.

- The soil should have a pH level between 6.5 and 7.0 and should be well-draining. Naturally, add some compost and fertilizer to the potting mix in your container before planting. Spinach needs as many nutrients as possible.

- Water the seeds regularly to keep the soil moist until they start germinating. Be careful not to drench them. Always water whenever you feel the topsoil around them getting dry.

Of course, you should thin out the leaves to make more room for the spinach for growth and early maturation.

Radishes

To enjoy some harvest quickly, then consider planting some radish in your garden. This is a great veggie that does not take long to grow or harvest. They not only do well in small spaces, but they also have a great flavor. Nobody dislikes the crunchy taste of a freshly picked garden radish.

In fact, they are an excellent veggie for you to begin your gardening journey with. Plus, you can use them for training your kids on the joy of gardening. Children can grow radishes and start seeing the fruit of their hard work in as little as seven days.

There are more varieties of radishes than you can imagine. The best ones to consider for your garden are the Cherry Belle (also called Red Globes), White Icicle, Chinese Red Meat, Black Radish, White Radish, Daikon, Snowball, and French Breakfast.

Radishes can tolerate most temperature levels but may bolt to seed if the temp is too high. They also grow in different soils. But to get the best result, plant your radishes in a thoroughly composted potting mix. A mix of loamy and sandy soil is the best for this sweet veggie. Your soil should have a pH between 5.8 and 6.8.

The soil should be well-drained because radishes don't function well with wet feet. Add sufficient high-quality fertilizer to the mix before planting.

Radishes like plenty of sunlight, but they also like partial shade when the temp is too high. Plant them near taller veggies like tomatoes, beans, and peas. Find a sunny windowsill with afternoon shade for your radish container to sit.

Never grow them in the full shade because all their energy and nutrients will be expended towards leaf growth. Rotate the crops to prevent disease.

Besides the ten vegetables explained in-depth above, other veggies you can plant in an indoor garden are:

- Potatoes
- Cauliflower
- Garlic
- Broccoli
- Avocado
- Microgreens
- Mushrooms
- Dwarf Beans
- Scallions
- Eggplant
- English Peas
- Kale
- Swiss Chard
- Sprouts
- Arugula
- Parsley
- Parsnip

There are several others apart from these, but you can get started with some here and then move on to experimenting with other types and varieties.

Chapter 7: Growing Herbs Indoors

Herbs are some of the easiest plants to grow indoors, as long as you know the right things to do. The key to building a successful indoor herb garden is to understand the growing requirements of the herbs you want and give them exactly what they need. It's simple and straightforward. Before discussing the exact herbs you can grow in your garden, there are some things to know about growing herbs.

The first is that herbs need very strong light. The more light you have in the growing environment, the more you will like the results of your herb plants. Many people don't know this, but the more intense light the herb garden gets, the stronger the flavors.

Growing your herbs under a very bright light gives them the best flavor possible. Besides that, you also know that light is crucial to plants' growth, and herbs are not excluded. In general, herbs need 6 to 8 hours of light directly from the sun.

So, always place your containers in a bright, sunny window or any other location that can be considered a sunroom. These are the ideal locations for growing herbs indoors. South-facing windows are the best overall choice. You can place a small table or bench in front of the window and then arrange your herb containers on it.

Do this if your windowsill cannot comfortably accommodate the pots.

Suppose you don't have a sunroom or an ideally sunny location. In that case, you'd need additional artificial lights to supplement whatever natural sunlight your herbs get from their location. A simple led or fluorescent bulb from your local hardware store is all you need if you aren't growing more than one or two herb pots.

Ideally, the temperature for growing most herbs indoors is between 67 and 70 degrees, which is excellent for most home environments. If you, at any point, want to slow your herb plants' growth, you can reduce the temperature to 60 or 65 degrees. Some herbs want a dormant period.

Herbs also prefer a slow, thorough, and infrequent watering schedule. Always let the planters dry out between watering. Examine the soil with your fingers if it is at least 2 inches dry below the top, indicating a need for moisture. But this generally depends on the size of the pot.

Don't worry about the soul becoming too dry to where it harms your plants. Even when the topsoil dries out quickly, there is usually enough moisture at the middle and bottom of the soil.

Infrequent watering gets the roots to grow deeper in the search for water. It is one way of ensuring the plants have a healthy root system.

Also, don't water your herbs too quickly, as this can push water right through the planter and out the drainage holes before the soil can retain the moisture. So, always water your herbs slowly.

You need not water your herbs daily, but follow a regular schedule three times per week. Depending on your home's humidity level, this could even be two times weekly. Some situations that may cause your herbs to require daily watering are:

- Small planting container. If the roots are filling up the whole pot, you need to switch to a bigger pot.
- Low humidity levels in your home.
- High-temperature levels. Too much heat can make the pots dry out much quicker. Move the herbs back to a location with more shade if the current location is too runny for them.

It's best to grow each herb in an individual pot. Combining herbs in one big container isn't recommended for indoor gardening. However, you can do that in an aero garden or outside gardening environment.

Usually, it's harder to create the right growing environment for several herbs in one pot unless you have the perfect environmental conditions. Planting in separate containers is the key to getting the flexibility you need for an indoor herb garden.

Doing that allows you to meet each herb's needs individually. If you still want to plant some herbs together, you can get a multi-herb planter from a garden center around you. But that only works find temporarily. If you desire long-term success with your herb garden, the best thing you can do is provide each herb its own pot.

Now that you know the basics of indoor herb gardening, let's discuss the ten best herbs to include in your garden.

Basil

Basil is a favorite of many gardeners. It is a fan of warmth and full sun. So, place your basil pot in the sunniest location in your kitchen, with a temperature of up to 75 degrees. Basil is an annual plant, so don't sit its pot near drafty or cold windows. It will grow better in a southern-facing window.

This herb is most famous for making pesto sauce. Still, you can use it in tomato dishes, cheeses, and vegetables.

The Greek Miniature Basil is one variety you can grow indoors. It's a compact variety that grows around 6 inches tall. You can use it in the same recipes as the Sweet Basil variety. Another variety is the Spicy Globe Basil which grows up to 10 inches high under the right conditions.

You can also grow large basil varieties in your kitchen herb garden with little to no problem. But they may not attain their full height unless you use a large container and turn on supplemental grow lights. So, you need not worry about the basil taking over your home. Lemon Basil and Sweet Genovese Basil are two other varieties that grow perfectly in indoor growing conditions.

With sufficient lighting, you can harvest your basil in as little as six weeks. If you have many recipes to use the herb with, start as many plants as you can. You can grow them together in a single, huge container to save space.

Cilantro

You can either love or hate the taste of fresh cilantro. There are no in-betweens. This herb has a powerful aroma and a peppery zing that makes it great for spicy recipes. You can use cilantro on sauces, stir-fried dishes, and salsas. It is popular in Asian, Mexican, and Mediterranean recipes.

Almost all the varieties of cilantro are suitable for growing indoors. The Calypso cilantrois variety particularly grows up to 18 inches tall. Another variety to watch out for is the Santo. Both varieties are bolt-resistant, which means they will give you a longer yield before the seeds set.

Cilantro herb prefers full sun or mild shade, so the ideal location is an eastern or southern-facing window. Harvesting can start in as little as 3 to 4 weeks. Early harvest promotes bushier cilantro plants.

Chives

Chives is a popular perennial herb with which you are probably familiar. It is in the same family as onions. Chives grow in clumps of shallow stems that are meant to be divided every three years. The taste of chive and its compact nature is all the reason you need to add it to your herb garden!

The crunchy texture makes this herb excellent for instant use. They can be added to omelets, cheeses, and soups and used as toppings on baked potatoes. You can plant any chive variety indoors, but the two most popular ones are the Onion and Garlic Chives.

Chives should be placed in an area with partial shade or full sun, like the southern or eastern-facing window. Compared to most herbs, chives like having moist soil. They are usually not ready for harvest until about 90 days after starting seed.

Dill

Dill differs from the dill seeds used in pickling. And this distinction is made through its other name Dillweed. This herb has naturally feathery leaves that take the shape of small fans. It is used in sauces, cheeses, salads, mustard and can be combined with butter or lemon on potatoes and fishes. An excellent indoor variety of Dill weed is the Fern Leaf Dill, which grows 18 inches high.

Dill grows well in partial or full sun, so a southern-facing window is just right for it. If planting from seed, try fitting three seedlings in an 8 inches wide container to grow in small bunches. That will give you a bountiful harvest.

You can start harvesting your dill once it sprouts up to 5 true leaves.

Oregano

Oregano is an herb with mildly hairy grayish-green leaves in the shape of an oval. It has a bushy habit, and that means it is a good herb to grow indoors. This herb is a favorite in Greek and Italian cuisine, so you might want to plant some if you have some Italian recipes to try out. It can be used with garlic, lemon, and tomato-based dishes.

The Greek Oregano is the most known variety, and it grows 8 to 12 inches high under the right conditions. Like any herb, oregano enjoys direct sunlight. Place its pot in a sunny window for the best flavor and growth.

Starter plants give a much quicker harvest than seeds. So, reconsider starting oregano from seeds.

Mint

Everyone is familiar with mint, but not everyone knows it is an easy plant to grow indoors. Mint sprawls quickly, though, so always keep it in a separate planter to avoid overcrowding the remaining herbs in your kitchen.

You can use mint for various culinary purposes. It makes an excellent addition to beverages. It is also used in desserts, and most famously, in lamb with mint sauce. Overall, there is no reason you shouldn't have mint in your indoor herb garden.

Spearmint is the most popular variety of mint used for cooking, thanks to its clean minty taste. Other varieties to consider are Chocolate Mint and Peppermint.

Mint enjoys partial shade or the morning sun. An east-facing window is just perfect for growing your mint. The herb also prefers moister soil like the Oregano, so you need to water and spritz it more frequently than other herbs.

The easiest way to add mint to your garden is to buy the starter plants. It's better than trying to grow it from seed.

Parsley

Parsley needs a pot larger than most herb plants to grow well indoors. This is due to its elongated taproot. It is one of the three herbs that make up the Bouquet Garni. The other two are thyme and bay leaves.

Parsley's fresh, crispy taste makes it a favorite in almost any cuisine. Its leaves are used in different recipes. The stems can also add flavor to stocks.

The most popular variety is the Flat Leaf Parsley, which many gardeners agree has the best flavor. Curly parsley is also used in salads and as garnish. It has a nice flavor that is somewhat milder than the flat-leaf parsley. You can grow both in your garden, but make sure the flat-leaf variety gets the bigger container.

This herb grows well on a sunny windowsill, so place it in the East or south-facing window. It has a high tolerance for cooler temperatures and more moisture than most herbs. It is easy to start from seed, but germination can take 14 to 21 days on average.

Parsley germinates more quickly when you soak its seeds overnight. This is one trick that gardeners generally can't get enough of.

Sage

You cannot start an indoor herb garden without the herb called sage. It is a reputed member of the Salvia family that serves both culinary and ornamental purposes. Sage is popularly used as an ingredient in brown butter sauce. It also works in bread, cheeses, stuffing, and heavy meat and game.

Dwarf Garden Sage is an excellent variety for an indoor grow room. Its compact growth habit allows it to grow up to 10 inches high.

Sage likes full, bright sun. Therefore, only put it in a south-facing window. Note it is also a short-lived perennial, which means you will need to replace the seeds every couple of years.

Rosemary

Rosemary herb has a powerful, warm taste. It is a fragrant herb that can be added to any indoor garden. The key is to plant as little as possible to prevent rosemary from overpowering the more delicate herbs with its strong fragrance.

You can use rosemary when roasting and also with meats and vegetables. Most recipes require you to chop the leaves finely. But if you wish, you can use the whole sprig to impart the flavor into your dish and then remove it before serving your meal.

The most popular indoor variety is the Blue Boy Rosemary which has a compact habit. This variety grows up to 24 inches high and has a quite nice flavor.

Rosemary is a Mediterranean herb, meaning it wants full sun contact. Still, put it in a somewhat cooler location. Never allow the soil to dry out fully before you water it. Consider buying new plants instead of starting seeds to grow rosemary in your garden.

Thyme

Thyme is a must-have classic herb in any garden. Its low-growing, well-branching nature makes it grow equally well in outdoor and indoor gardens. You can add it to slow-steamed stews and soups and then remove it before serving. It goes perfectly with anything from meat to fish, poultry, and vegetable. It is an incredibly versatile herb plant.

By its nature, thyme is a compact herb, which means you can grow most varieties indoors. The Lemon thyme and English thyme varieties are the most commonly grown varieties indoors.

Thyme is easy to start from seed and relatively easy to care for. You can grow it in groups together in a single planter for a fuller and nicer effect. A 5-inch pot can accommodate five or more thyme seedlings.

Apart from these ten herbs, other varieties you can grow in your garden include:

- Lemongrass
- Garden Cress
- Catnip

- Lemon Balm
- Chervil
- Tarragon
- Bay Leaves

Mason jars are the perfect containers for creating a vertical herb garden in your kitchen. You can mark each herb jar with your label maker to make the herbs identifiable.

Chapter 8: Selecting Flowers to Grow Indoors

Whether you want flowers in your garden for aesthetic, culinary, or fragrant purposes, there are several options to choose from. You can make your indoor garden a purely aesthetic one by growing flowering plants only. However, the beauty of an indoor garden is usually in its diversity. So, it's best to have a combination of veggies, herbs, fruits, and flowers indoors.

Flowering plants add a definitive color, vibrancy, and scents to your home, and that is why they deserve to be in your garden. If you are worried that flowers are much harder to grow than other plants, don't worry.

The flowering plants here are some of the easiest to grow, and they perform incredibly well indoors. Some of these are edible, while others are purely for decorative purposes. Not only can flowers brighten your home and your mood, but they also add flavor and color to your dishes.

Many can garnish salads, soups, and desserts due to their range of nutrients and vitamins. If you are making body care items, you can even use some of your homegrown flowers to do that. It is important to know edible flowers from non-edible ones. So, there will be a tag to help you differentiate.

Calendula (edible)

Calendula, also called Calendula officinalis, is a flowering plant with bright yellow, gold, and orange flowers. It has a peppery taste that is quite distinctive. Calendula is used to add color to dishes, specifically rice, instead of saffron.

This flower has a longer blooming season than many others, which means you can grow it during winter. The petals can be used to add a dashing brightness to your summer salads. Calendula flowers may also be used to make tea with mild antiseptic and astringent properties.

It can be used to treat ulcers, cramps, and other gastrointestinal problems. Try combining it with another herb or flower to achieve the desired tea taste.

African Violet (non-edible)

This is one of the most popular flowering plants that grow well in an indoor garden. The African violet produces very beautiful flowers in shades of purple, white, and red. They bloom year-round, which means they will keep your home looking attractive no matter what season it is.

This flowering houseplant may not be high-maintenance, but the small, leafy plants do better when you put them in pots that let them absorb water from the bottom. Therefore, you need a 5 to 6 inches pot to grow them until they are mature.

To encourage the healthy growth of your African violet, eliminate dead leaves regularly and swap the pot for a bigger one once the plant starts getting bigger. Finally, don't overwater them because that can make them spot and turn brown. In extreme cases, they may even die off.

One thing about African violets is that they usually die off without warning after blooming and flourishing in a garden for several years.

Chrysanthemums (edible)

Chrysanthemums, also called mums for short, have a spicy and pungent smell that stands out from other flowers. They come in a variety of colors with equally various flavors. The most common are reds, yellows, and whites.

This plant can be added to rice dishes, stir-fries, and salads and can also serve an aesthetic value in your home. Mums do well with lots of sunlight and will generally grow healthy in well-drained soil.

Scented Geraniums (non-edible)

Geraniums are fragrant flowers. Their spikes make them one of the best-looking flowering plants you will ever see in any garden. Scented geranium has natural scented foliage, which differentiates it from many other fragrant plants.

There are different colors and scents, so watch out for your favorite ones when purchasing geranium from a nursery around you. Also, remember that the cultivars rarely bloom. Geraniums are grown mostly for their fragrant leaves.

These plants love the sunlight. They won't mind if you drench them in sunlight for as long as possible. You can place a container in your room if you have a south or east-facing window. Remember that they need direct exposure to the sun to bloom and thrive, so don't compromise the location for anything.

Begonia (non-edible)

You have probably seen Begonia flowers somewhere outside your home. Still, they come in a wide range of varieties that make them excellent plants for an indoor garden. Under the proper conditions, these plants will bloom almost daily.

Begonia is best placed in a very bright area, but you shouldn't leave it near a window as the drafts can cause damage. The colorful leaves add a splash of beauty to any room they are in, even when it's not the blooming season.

Some of the best varieties to grow are the hairy-leaved, angel-wing, and wax-leaved varieties. These have adapted to indoor and container gardening quite effortlessly.

Hibiscus (edible)

Hibiscus tea is made from the lush hibiscus flower, which comes in a purple, blueish, and pink hue. It is a huge source of Vitamin C and a common ingredient in different herbal teas. Thanks to its anti-inflammatory properties, it can soothe coughs, aching limbs, and headaches. You can use hibiscus flowers to make syrup, jam, and tea.

Bromeliad (non-edible)

This flowering plant bears a striking resemblance to pineapples but isn't eligible to be added to your edible garden. The flowers are quirky, bright, and colorful. The plants are compact and can fit comfortably in a container.

You can recognize a bromeliad from its basal rosettes and showy flowers, which come in a colorful assortment of pink, yellow, red, and orange. Many of the bromeliad varieties are air plants due to their tropical nature.

Air plants get their moisture from the atmosphere, so humidity plays a very important role in the growth of bromeliad flowers. However, this doesn't mean you shouldn't water them regularly. Just ensure you spritz the water between their leaves when you do water them. That way, they can take their time to absorb the moisture.

Chenille (non-edible)

Chenille is also called the red-hot cattail plant due to its bright, fur-like flowers. It is both a fast grower and a long bloomer, so you can have it in your home for a long time while doing very little work. You can grow chenille in your home during the colder months.

This plant tends to become partially dormant in colder seasons, so you will need grow lights to ensure it keeps blooming. Mist it with water and keep the humidity levels high if you want them to remain moist and keep thriving.

Some other flowering plants that will make great inclusions in your indoor flower garden are:

- Christmas Cactus
- Violet
- Pansies
- Nasturtiums
- Orchids
- Lily of the Valley
- Gardenia
- Passionflower
- Indoor Citrus
- Tasmanian Blue Gum
- Hoya Plant
- Bee Balm
- Tuberose
- Sweet Osmanthus
- Orange Jasmine
- Angel's Trumpet
- Plumeria
- Cuban Oregano
- Myrtus
- Miniature Rose
- Jasmine
- Spider Lily

Depending on why you want flowers in your garden, you can plant two or more of these in your home.

Chapter 9: Fruit Tree Options for Indoor Gardens

Why would anybody grow a fruit tree inside their home?

Well, why shouldn't they? If you have the available space, there is no reason you can't plant a fruit tree inside your home. There are many things to benefit from the clean air to the beautiful foliage. And more importantly, the fruits you won't have to buy from the grocery store.

The general belief about fruit trees is that they are impossible to grow indoors. After all, how could you hope to fit those tall and huge plants in your home? Contrary to popular belief, there are lots of fruit trees that are growable indoors.

Dwarf fruit tree varieties are made specifically for growing in containers inside the home. They are appealing, and they offer you a nice change from the usual philodendron and spider plant.

If you've never seen a dwarf fruit tree, they are grafted into a stock that enables them to stay small and compact. But some varieties can grow larger than is normal for an indoor garden. So, you must keep the size manageable with regular pruning.

These days, you can find dwarf fruit trees anywhere from your local nursery to garden centers. If you can't find the variety you want in your local store, you can find anyone you want on the Amazon online store. Most varieties you find will grow well in containers.

If you get the tree from your local nursery, make sure you repot it immediately, especially if the roots are cramped. There, gently prune the roots and loosen the soil before putting the tree in a new container. Use a pot that is slightly bigger than the original container.

If you purchase your tree online, it will likely come bare, meaning it won't be planted in soil. You will need to inspect the roots and prune the damaged parts before planting them in a container.

So, which fruit trees would be good to have in your indoor garden? Find out below.

Strawberries

Not everyone is familiar with the ease of growing strawberries indoors. They are some of the easiest fruits to grow inside your home because they need little sunlight. Plus, they have a compact size, so you can easily plant a bunch of them in one container and then place them on a windowsill with the least amount of direct sunlight.

The normal temperature in your home should be near the ideal temp for growing strawberries. Some varieties do well in hot temperatures as well. If your home tends to get frosty during a particular season, you will need to keep the temperature at the required level so your strawberries can survive and thrive.

The plants dry out quite quickly, so watch out for this. Check them every day and water or mist them according to their needs. Keep the humidity levels high so they can absorb moisture from around them.

Lemon

You may be surprised to learn that lemon is one of the easiest fruits to grow indoors, but that is a fact. Naturally, you can only grow a dwarf variety for your garden. Some of the more ideal options are Lisbon, Meyer, and Ponderosa lemon dwarf tree. Do not grow a standard lemon variety because, eventually, you won't be able to fit it in your home.

You shouldn't save seed to grow lemon as any seed from a shop is more than likely to be from a full-size tree. Plus, it sometimes takes up to 6 years for a seed-planted tree to start bearing fruits. If you have the patience, go for it! It's usually worth the wait.

But you are better off buying a dwarf variety that is already growing. Most experts recommend buying one that is two to three years old. These will grow and mature much faster, and you can start reaping the fruits of your labor.

Figs

The best variety of figs to grow indoors is the Negro Largo. It performs well in an enclosed space. It does best well-lit location, but you have to shield it from direct sunlight. Temperature affects the size, so you need to keep it between 65 and 70 degrees to regulate your fully mature fig tree size. Most varieties only need you to feed them a few times during planting season.

Bananas

Like everyone else, you probably like bananas. They pump us with energy and are generally good for our health. In their natural habitat, bananas grow as tall as 30 feet. Fortunately, there are dwarf varieties that can be grown indoors. Add that to pruning, and you won't have to worry about a banana tree towering over you in your home.

You need only to purchase a sucker or corm from the plant store and plant it in a container filled with loamy soil. Then, place it in an area with at least 6 hours of daily sunlight. Water every three days and add some fertilizer once every week.

Some varieties to consider are the Super Dwarf Cavendish, Dwarf Lady Finger, Dwarf Jamaican, Dwarf Brazilian, etc.

Mulberry

A bush of mulberries is an excellent inclusion in any indoor fruit garden. In the wild, mulberry bushes can grow as tall as 10 feet. However, the dwarf version is usually between 4 to 5 feet, which means you can plant mulberry indoors.

The impressive thing about a mulberry bush is it can produce up to four harvests in a year, which means you are sure to get a sufficient number of mulberries to munch on! To grow and thrive, mulberries just need around 6 hours of partial sunlight. You can place the pot on a windowsill or in front of the window itself.

One problem to look out for is that mulberry bushes dry out very quickly. This can happen even more quickly in an enclosed environment. Therefore, you must regularly water your mulberry bush while also applying some much-needed fertilizer.

Other fruit trees you can grow indoors are:

- Lime
- Berries blueberry, blackberry, and raspberry
- Citrus
- Cucamelon

- Pineapple
- Orange

Many other fruits are growable inside, but you can begin your journey with some of these to build a diverse indoor garden within your home. Don't just stop at these veggies, fruits, flowers, and herbs discussed, though.

Research more about unusual varieties and choose those that seem like they will complement your garden well. Try new plants and varieties even if you are unfamiliar with them. That is the surest way to create the beautiful, diverse garden that is the dream of many growers. The good thing is that you can still do all these while gardening on a budget.

Chapter 10: Getting Started on Your Indoor Garden

Now that you are familiar with the fundamentals of indoor gardening, let's move on to setting up your garden. This chapter will detail how you can plant and arrange your garden to produce the aesthetic result you want for your home.

Before you get to this part, you must have settled on a design. Decide if you want a vertical design, shelves, or other designs and styles explained in chapter three. Then, sketch out a rough portrait of how you want your home to look when you are finished planting and arranging your fruit trees, herbs, flowers, and veggies. Then you can start the practical side.

As a new gardener, try to keep things small. You might be tempted to go all out, but that can become overwhelming if you haven't tried gardening before. Try to grow one or two pots of fruits, herbs, flowers, and veggies, respectively, before you go all in.

Quickly, let's run through the things you need to do to get to this point again:

- Choose the perfect location. The most logical choice is inside and around your kitchen. The closer your herbs and veggies are as you cook, the likelier you will include them in your recipes. That also makes harvesting easier.

- Choose the plants. Select your favorite houseplants and purchase them from any local or online store. Select the ones you consume the most regularly. More importantly, make sure the plants you choose have similar growing requirements. That will make your job much easier, especially if you have limited space.

- Get the different containers required to grow the plants you want in your garden. Don't forget to get varying sizes based on the growing tendencies of the plants.

After choosing your plants, the next step is to plant the crops inside their designated containers. You have already learned how to create high-quality potting soil for your different plants. Follow the instructions on your seed packets to create the potting mix according to the requirements of each plant variety.

If you want an Instagram-worthy setting for your garden, remember that you can create that. Anyone can arrange their indoor space to look like something out of an interior décor magazine with the right tips and guidelines. Some things you need to set up the perfect plant-laden living space of your dream are texture, height, and layering. As long as you understand these three things and some general rules of thumb, you are good to go.

Indoor plants are generally more challenging to arrange to create a beautiful setting. Not all plants have similar requirements. For instance, you might think that two plants will look good together in the same area, only to discover that you can't grow them around each other.

Some plants look great in smaller, darker spaces, while others' beauty will only shine through if you put them in an open space. Therefore, you have to familiarize yourself with all these basics before you start arranging your plants.

Good arrangement does not only improve your interior appearance; it can also impact the health and growth of your house plants positively.

The first rule of thumb used in setting up an indoor garden is always to avoid grouping even-numbered plants together. Paired items give an awkwardly formal look, and you don't want that in your home.

A much better combination is achieved through a group of three, but you still need to ensure there is an odd number of plants in each grouping. Here are some things to note when creating a plant cluster:

- Do not put plants that are of uniform height in the same group. That will only blend them all together. Try putting one plant that is noticeably taller in the middle of each grouping.

- Find a commonality when grouping plants together. For example, you can arrange plants with dense leaves together. Color is another common feature you can use to arrange them. As long as every plant in a collection has one uniform trait, they won't look out of place next to each other.

Textures are another important thing to consider when creating visual interest. It does not just apply to furniture and décor, but plants as well. With the varying foliage textures, plants can help establish variation within a living space.

When arranging your indoor plants, you need to think in terms of contrasting textures. This means that you pair coarse with smooth, minimal with detailed, and so on.

If your home décor is minimalistic, you can go for plants with detailed appearances to complement the look of your home. If you have a textured home with blankets, layered rugs, and the likes, then you need plants with refined leaves in your home. That will balance things out for you.

You also need to learn to take advantage of your plants' height when arranging them. Try exploring the parts of your home at eye level or taller. While you can only display tall plants on ground level, smaller plants provide an opportunity to try out different heights.

Below are helpful tips to get your plants off the ground:

- Place trailing plants on shelves so their vines can grow out and give your indoor space an attractive jungle look.

- Put medium-sized plants too big for shelves and too small to serve as focal points on their own plant stand. That will make them stand out from others.

As you arrange those plants, check out the natural direction of their foliage. This is called the leading line, and you can take advantage of it to draw attention to specific parts of your home. Leading lines work better with plants whose leaves trail down or point upwards.

- The Zanzibar Gem and Snake Plant are two plants with leaves that go upwards. You can use them near your wall arts to call attention to them when they start pointing upwards.

- Plants from the philodendron or Pothos family's vines trail downward. You can display these in your bookshelves to draw attention to the fireplace.

Although it's tempting to match the color of your plant stands to your furniture and coffee table, you need not do that. Aspire to have some variation to create spice in your garden.

You can add color to your home without creating a rather dramatic or hodge-podge look by following the three rules of thumb explained above. Typically, you should have a primary, secondary, and accent color in the space.

Some ways you can achieve a more colorful look for your space include:

- Switching up the container colors. Don't just settle for a basic white or black color. Add more colors to your planters, even if it's a neutral one.

- Try different variegated plants so you can have some colorful leaves as well.

When designing, you need to remember your plants' needs. If you don't arrange the plants in a way that meets their basic needs, the entire space will eventually take on an ugly look. So, remember this as you set up and design your very own garden!

Chapter 11: Maintaining Your Indoor Garden

You must have picked up some plant care tips from every chapter so far in this book. But here, you will find an in-depth breakdown of the best practices for taking care of and maintaining an indoor garden while dealing with minimal problems.

Water

As established several chapters earlier, water is essential for taking care of your indoor plants. It is also crucial to the maintenance of your garden. The potting soil mix you use for planting should neither be dry nor wet. Instead, it should be kept moist at all times.

Of course, there are always exceptions to rules. Some thick-leafed plants perform their best when you let the potting mix dry out in between watering. If you keep the soil too damp or dry, their roots may begin to rot and subsequently lead to the dormancy or death of the plants.

You can tell when a plant needs watering by the texture of the soil. If it suddenly becomes cracked with a lighter color, that is a cry for moisture. After watering your plants, pick up the container and try to assess its weight.

After doing this a few times, you should be able to determine when your plant needs freshwater by picking up the container and gauging its weight. Of course, you can also stick your finger inside the soil to check the moisture below the surface level. It's better to use a handheld meter for larger plants.

Dehydration is a problem many plants often have to face because of neglectful owners. Never allow your plants to get to where the soil starts pulling from the container's edge, or the leaves start wilting. These are signs of dehydration, and they may indicate that your roots are already damaged.

Check out the signs below to know when your crops are underwatered:

- Transparent leaves
- Premature leaf or flower droppings
- Brown and curled leaves edges
- Delayed leaf growth

Overwatering is just as detrimental to plants as dehydration. It can force the air from your soil and open up the door for root-killing diseases to invade. In fact, some experts believe that overwatering is the leading houseplant killer.

Check out the signs below to determine if you are overwatering your plants:

- Both young and old leaves start falling off
- Mold forms on the soil surface
- Roots turn stinky and mushy beneath the soil
- Extra water standing at the base of the planting container

- Leaves develop brown decayed patches.

Suppose you lead a busy lifestyle, and you aren't sure you can keep up with the watering schedules of your plants. In that case, you can set up a self-watering device that will draw water from an available bowl into your plants' roots.

Room temp water from the tap is good enough for most indoor plants. It does not matter if there is fluoride or chlorine in the water. Plants generally love melted snow and rainwater. But don't use softened water too often as it may contain sodium.

You can water your plants from the bottom-up or top-down choose whatever watering style works best for you. Try to moisten your entire soil mass while keeping the foliage damp. There should be water dripping from the drainage holes drilled at the base of your planter.

Fertilizer

Fertilizing your plants is a huge part of the maintenance process. Every time you water a plant, it automatically leaks some nutrients from the soil. Even when that doesn't happen, plants deplete their nutrients reserve very quickly.

Unlike outdoor plants, houseplants don't have a stable source of nutrient replenishment. The only way they get that is when you feed them quality fertilizer. So, that is something you must do as regularly as required.

In general, you should fertilize your plants once every month once they start growing and flowering. Only withdraw fertilizer when a plant is dormant or growing really slow. If a certain plant shows signs of slow growth or yellow-green color, it might mean it needs more fertilizer.

But it could also mean that the plant needs less water or more light. Therefore, take your time to analyze your plants' conditions before you give them more fertilizer. Giving plant food to a plant that does not need it may just be worse than feeding it nothing.

There are different types of fertilizers but only use organic and specific to indoor plants. Synthetic fertilizers are more likely to burn your plants, so go for natural ones. Still, applying the exact amount required is very important.

Note that low-light plants won't require the same amount of fertilizer as the medium-light and high-light ones.

First, apply a quarter of the recommended amount of fertilizer on the seed packet label once a month. Then, watch out for changes in overall plant color. If it becomes lighter, start applying the fertilizer twice a month. Conversely, if the leaves become dark green and small with longer space between them, reduce the rate at which you apply fertilizer.

Note: Synthetic fertilizers build up soluble salt that can form a crusty pile of salts on your soil surface. Get rid of that layer and leach the soil with enough water every six weeks to prevent toxic salt buildup. Excess salt can make your plants susceptible to pest and disease attacks.

Repotting

Over time, some of your thriving plants might need a larger planter, especially if they grow the right way. Sometimes, you just need to change the potting mix for some fresh soil. The best time to repot plants is when they have just begun growing. Healthy and vibrant root growth means that your plants will adjust to their new containers very quickly.

Use a soilless medium designed specifically for indoor plants when it is time to re-pot. Then, make sure the new container is bigger than the previous one. The size difference should be minimal as a huge pot can cause wet feet and root rot.

Pruning and Harvesting

Naturally, you want to enjoy a bountiful and successful harvest after the growing season. While most people are consumed with ways to reduce maintenance and get more yield with less work, they often overlook one simple thing pruning. Some of the things that planters overlook are rewarding in ways that they rarely realize.

Pruning may seem counterintuitive to a successful harvest, but it is actually vital to the process. If you don't take pruning seriously, you may find that your harvest at the end of a growing season is nothing near what you wanted.

To clarify, pruning isn't the same as harvesting, even though both involve removing bits by bits of your plants. However, you can generally combine both for most plants. The main objective of pruning is to encourage plant growth, while harvesting is done to remove the parts that are ready to use. Some plants, such as ornamental flowers, need to be pruned even if you won't harvest them.

Pruning protects your plants' health and helps to control their shape and height for your convenience. When you remove a stem between two leaves in some plants, more stems grow in their place.

Rather than growing narrow and tall, plants need to grow outwards. You may prune your plants repeatedly for a contrasting reason. In a plant such as a tomato, you may have to remove the "suckers" to keep the plant straight and tidy. That will also keep them from bushing out.

By doing that, a plant can expend less of its energy on growth and more on fruiting. It also helps to keep some plants from breaking under their own weights.

How to tip plants successfully:

- Start pruning as early as possible so you can have a decent amount of produce in the long term.

- Do not prune over 1/3 of your plants. It's much harder for plants to sustain themselves when you've removed the bulk of their stems and leaves. So, you need to be as gentle as possible.

- Always wait until there are at least three sets of leaves on the stem before pruning any plant.

- Use a sharp pruner because blunt ones can cause damage and infection. Refer to chapter 4 to remember why you shouldn't use a dull or blunt pruner on your plants.

- Only remove stems that are above the leaves when pruning. That will ensure that the remaining attached buds have room to grow.

- For bushy plants, cut the top 2 to 3 inches of the stem. The plants will naturally grow new stems laterally.

- Follow an inwards and outwards pattern by removing any leaves blocking inner growth from receiving light and removing inner growth which isn't receiving light.

Harvesting is done when a plant is at its peak. You can tell this from the scent or flavor. Like pruning, you must be careful to remove as little of your plants as possible. Otherwise, the plants can't sustain themselves.

For example, lettuce is a hardy plant, which means you can harvest it in various ways. A common style is the "haircut" practice which involves snipping the leaves off at the very top of the plants. This technique is quicker for gardeners with plenty of plants to harvest.

Another technique is single leaf harvesting which involves removing the mature leaves and leaving the younger ones to grow further. This technique is great if you have few plants or just want to pick a couple of veggies for your salad.

The single leaf harvesting method can be used on lettuce, kale, arugula, and many other leafy ones.

These plants must be regularly harvested. Otherwise, they can become bitter. Some may even bolt without proper maintenance, and once bolting starts, the leaves become smaller and inedible. This means that the surest way to get a sustained harvest is to keep your veggies, herbs, fruits, and edible flowers trimmed.

Pests and Diseases

If you neglect your houseplants without inspecting and checking them out regularly, you leave them susceptible to pests and diseases. Not only can these affect your leaves and flowers, but they also damage the stems and roots. Therefore, prevention is much better than elimination.

The first step to avoiding pests and diseases in your indoor garden is to purchase clean and healthy seeds and plants. This very basic step reduces the risk of infection on new and existing plants.

If you aren't certain about the health of a particular plant, quarantine it from the garden and wait to see if there'd be any improvements. Doing the above is better than introducing a defective plant to your grow room, where it can infect other plants.

When watering your plants, inspect them and pinch off any dead flowers you see. If you notice a slight problem, treat it immediately to ensure it doesn't get out of hand. In addition, only use a healthy and clean potting mix. Do not keep cuttings off plants with questionable health.

Remember that many indoor plants will not grow to their full potential if you don't feed them regularly. Most gardeners never forget to water their plants, but many have trouble remembering to feed them with nutrients.

Plants become diseased when they don't get the nutrients they need. Plus, they have a better chance of fighting any disease or infestation when you regularly feed them a balanced nutritional diet. Be careful not to overfeed them as this can make the potting mix toxic, and that, in turn, kills the plants or slows down their growth considerably.

Here are some common plant problems that can cause pest and disease infestation.

- Variegated-leaved plants become green when you don't put them in an area with good lighting conditions. Flowering plants start losing their leaves when the soil is too dry, or the light level is insufficient.

- When in a draft, healthy leaves fall off the plants after first curling at the edges. A too-high temperature or too-dry soil can cause lower leaves to become brown and crispy.

- Flower buds fall off when lighting is insufficient or the air is too dry.

Some of the most common houseplant pests to watch out for are:

- Aphids: These pests cause stagnant growth and yellowish and distorted leaves. They also leave a sticky, black substance on your plants. They can cause and spread incurable viruses in your garden.

- Cyclamen mites: These can harm your strawberries, begonia flower, African violets, geranium, and other plants. The damage they cause is typically unnoticeable until the havoc is wrecked. They turn the leaves darker, curled, streaked, and distorted.

• Caterpillars: These typically affect certain vegetables and leaves. They eat holes in your leaves. You may not have to worry about them if they are only harmful.

• Earwigs: These garden pests have a frightening look, but they are generally harmless to people. Still, they can be a menace in the garden. They have a knack for chewing on vegetables, flowers, herbs, and other plants. You can identify an infestation of earwig by the holes and edges they leave on the petals and leaves.

• Mealybugs: The enclosed environment makes your indoor plants vulnerable to mealybugs. These are pests that leave a whitish cotton-resembling residue on the plants they attack. The cotton can be found on the leaves and stems.

• Scale insects: Scale pose a problem to any indoor plants. They suck the nutrients out of plants, leaving them susceptible to diseases. They thrive best in dry environments.

The most common diseases houseplants are prone to are:

- Leaf spot
- Root rot
- Botrytis
- Rust
- Blackleg
- Sooty mold
- Powdery mildew

Pest and disease infestation is not usually common in indoor gardens, but be on the lookout for any problem. You need not know plenty about the insects and diseases that can affect your plants. Just check out for them.

If you ever need to treat your plants, you can apply the chemicals in several ways. The most common technique is to dilute the insecticide in clean water and pour it inside your spray bottle. Then, you just need to spritz the garden. Dusting your plants with insecticide powder can also help eliminate pests. But this method may leave a messy residue of dirt on your plants.

Remember, caring for and maintaining your plants go well beyond watering and fertilizing them. Always be on the lookout for anything out of the ordinary. An early nip in the bud can save your plants and garden as a whole!

Conclusion

This book has explained many aspects of indoor gardening and the techniques that will succeed for you. But the fact, your success is more dependent on you than the techniques you've learned. Ultimately, you need to be willing to play around with a mix of veggies, fruits, flowers, and herbs.

Indoor Gardening is meant to be an introductory guide to gardening within your apartment or home, especially for those who haven't experimented with growing their crops before.

Over time, you will learn more about plants and gain more expertise as you try your hands at different varieties and systems. Gardening is not a one-system thing. You can continuously improve your knowledge and even come up with techniques on your own. Good luck!

Part 2: Vertical Gardening

A Beginner's Guide to Growing Fruit, Vegetables, Herbs and Flowers on a Living Wall and How to Create an Urban Garden in Small Spaces

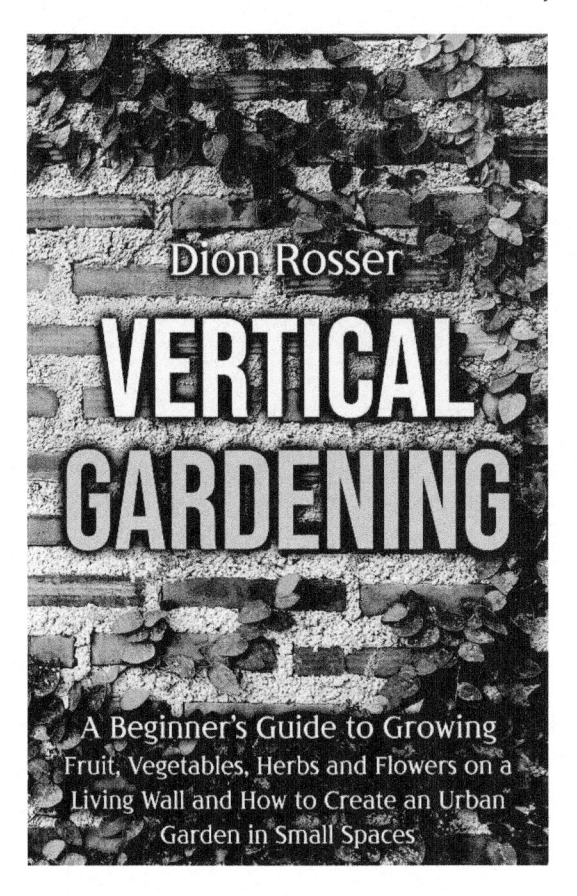

Introduction

This book will introduce you to the world of vertical gardening and living walls, preparing you to take on the exciting challenge of creating your very own. You'll learn what vertical gardening is, how to start and maintain your own garden, and how to ensure a successful experience on your new ecologically friendly journey.

Not only is this book easy to read, but it's also full of the latest information on the subject and a hands-on approach that will help guide you from the very first step. Each chapter will take you through a simple step-by-step approach, teaching you everything you will need to learn before taking off on your own. Each chapter includes instructions on achieving certain tasks and will guide you towards making the right decision for you and your new lifestyle.

Gardening has its challenges, but vertical gardening has a few advantages that may help first-time gardeners, making it the perfect gardening method to start with. You may simply prefer this form of gardening because of a lack of space, but you will soon learn about all it has to offer.

This is vertical gardening 101 and is perfect for those who have no prior knowledge and want to learn about everything, starting with the simplest details.

This is a beginner's guide to growing fruit, vegetables, herbs, or flowers on a living wall or vertical garden, and it will teach you everything you need to know. Besides instructions, you will also find simple DIY tutorials that you can tackle for a more cost-effective take on this project. This book is for every type of beginner.

Chapter 1: The Benefits of Vertical Gardens and Living Walls

As the world has been forced to deal with new and unprecedented circumstances, more and more people are finding themselves working from home. Many of those people have picked up an array of new hobbies, one of which is gardening. Creative people have found solutions to make life easier in every area of our daily lives, so why not explore some modern gardening methods? You've likely heard by now about vertical storage, where storage units are built against walls in every (previously unused) corner of our homes. They're not just space savers; they're also aesthetically pleasing.

Vertical gardens and living walls are the next best thing in gardening; they're the new "vertical storage." Soon, more and more people will adopt this new method. Liberating more space on your countertops, desks, floors, or even balcony and terrace should be on your to-do list. And if you don't do it for the aesthetics, do it for the practicality of these beautiful, living, green walls.

Imagine enjoying a glass of wine or a meal with friends or family while surrounded by a luscious canopy of greenery. Who needs a new lick of paint when you can have the different textures, colors, and scents of a garden envelop you in your very own indoor oasis? An oasis that you grew yourself!

What are Vertical Gardens and Living Walls?

To put it simply, vertical gardens or living walls are exactly what they sound like. They are gardens that can cover entire walls, unlike the typical horizontal gardens we're accustomed to. Vertical gardens are also known as living walls because the plants are real living organisms. You might have even heard of moss walls; moss is a plant commonly used to create living walls.

These gardens may be entirely hydroponic, which is the method of growing plants in nutrient-rich water rather than earth.

These gardens can be as small or as large as you want, and they can contain anything from plants to flowers or even fruit and vegetables. What they all have in common is that they are vertical structures, mostly green, and are sure to add a unique and practical twist to your space. Besides making a great décor statement, they're also incredibly beneficial for different reasons. Find out below why they are beneficial to your home, your health, and more.

Why are Vertical Gardens Beneficial?

There are plenty of benefits to growing a vertical garden or living wall, and some of them might surprise you.

Take Up Less Space

One of the most obvious advantages to vertical growing is space. You don't need as much space to grow plants, and therefore you can grow even more than you would in a horizontal garden. You can take advantage of even the smallest outdoor areas in your home by growing your own vegetables or herbs with the simple use of a vertical garden. You can also have a raised garden in non-traditional areas like a balcony or on a wall inside your home.

You Don't Need a Green Thumb

While you'll still need to take care of your living wall garden, vertical gardens' upkeep is less taxing than traditional ones. Because they're vertical, common problems that plague traditional gardens like weeds and pests won't be as much of a problem. In fact, soil-borne diseases won't be a problem at all in a hydroponic setup. So, even if you don't feel very confident growing plants, this can be an easier start for you. They still require some maintenance, though, which we will discuss further along in the book.

Easier Harvesting

If you're anything like me, the idea of squatting in a garden for hours looking for bugs and harvesting crops does not excite you. This is another benefit to growing a vertical garden, as there is no need to add strain to your body when collecting the vegetables or herbs you've grown. This is because most of your crops will be at hip-to-shoulder level. This allows even elderly people to create their own garden and grow produce without any help from others.

Reduce Noise

Vertical gardens act as a sound barrier and reduce noise coming into your space from the outside. They can even be more effective than traditional construction materials used to soundproof space.

This is why they are sometimes used in offices located in busy streets or apartments facing an avenue with a lot of traffic.

Reduce Temperature

Besides acting as a great soundproofing barrier, living walls also do wonders for areas with high temperatures. Plants lower the temperature of the space around them through a process called transpiration. This process works even during the highest temperature peaks. Imagine a cosmopolitan city with skyscrapers and busy streets; the heat in such places gets trapped between buildings, and even pedestrians can feel the effect. That same city carpeted in beautiful green walls would have an entirely different effect as these living walls would help lower the temperature by a considerable degree. Growing living walls in such places can prove beneficial, especially in years to come, as climate change becomes more of an issue.

Promote Biodiversity

Having plants and flowers around helps preserve ecosystems, and these living walls are no exception. You'll be promoting biodiversity in your area, allowing bees and other beneficial insects to thrive locally. Some living walls installed on buildings even include habitat boxes so that insects and small animals have shelter within those walls.

Placing Your New Vertical Garden

Vertical gardens or living walls are a great addition to dwellings such as townhouses, apartments, office spaces, building facades, hospitals, and more. To onlookers, they are visually appealing, of course, but we also know that they serve several ecological and health purposes.

Townhouses

One benefit of growing a vertical garden in a townhouse is that it's an attractive way to conceal your patio area or a backyard from your next-door neighbors. A freestanding vertical garden helps add some privacy to your outdoor space while also keeping the area looking fresher and quieter. This is especially beneficial during the summers or if you live near busy streets.

Apartments

If you live in an apartment, having your own vertical garden can help bring the outside in, make your space feel cozier, and improve air quality, especially if you live in a big city. Also, if you have a small balcony, you can still grow your own produce because vertical gardens don't take up much floor space. This will allow you to make the most of your balcony's space and turn it into your very own green oasis.

Office Spaces/Workspace

A living wall can guarantee happier, more productive employees and better air quality in an office space. Since plants reduce temperatures, companies will spend less on air-conditioning during the warmer months, thereby reducing energy costs. Moreover, by having an attractive and more relaxing environment, your office will catch clients' attention, which will lead to more business.

Building Facades

If you're considering building a large-scale vertical garden, a full-scale building facade is one way to go. Because vertical gardens are living things, no two green facades will look the same. This means your building will have its own truly unique look. Carpeted by the beauty of this natural facade, your building is sure to stand out and draw positive attention from every onlooker. Of course, the other benefits mentioned above apply here as well; the façade will help lower the temperature in the surrounding area, produce oxygen, and improve people's moods.

Hospitals

Another possible location for living walls, and perhaps the most surprising one of all, is hospitals. Studies in the International Journal of Environmental Research and Public Health have shown that being surrounded by a calming green environment helps patients recover faster and increases their pain tolerance. You may experience the same soothing effect when out in nature, whether it be a hike in the woods or a picnic near a lake or waterfall. The natural elements contribute to stress relief and healing. This is why living walls are a great addition to hospital wards, especially ones that cater to patients with chronic illnesses.

The idea behind the living walls in all of the places previously mentioned is that they can improve your quality of life through their beauty or practicality. Due to their adaptable size, you can even set up your vertical garden in your bathroom, provided that there's a window. Regardless of where you choose to build it, a vertical garden is sure to be a unique design idea for your home or space.

Vertical Gardens Are Trendy!

If you're still not convinced, telling you vertical gardens or living walls are very "in" right now might just do the trick. There are many reasons why vertical gardens are trendy at the moment, but I'll name a few for you.

Wow-Factor

First and foremost, they're unexpected. People don't expect to find a tall wall of green vegetation indoors. They offer that wow factor that many people love. A hotel lobby or office won't usually have a living wall, but when they do, you're surprised and happy to see them. The living wall makes you feel welcome and instantly more relaxed. Even outside a building, looking up to see a fun, green facade instead of a blank expanse of concrete block is also unexpected. Imagine New York City, a concrete jungle, with new and improved buildings carpeted in beautiful shades of green. It wouldn't be just unexpected and relaxing; it would be breathtaking. Living walls make the urban greys come to life.

Indoor-Outdoor Flow

In your own home, vertical gardens can bring a touch of the outdoors to your indoor space. For those living in small apartments without outside space, like a balcony, having a vertical garden inside your home brings in the aura of life you can find only outside. Plants create a peaceful atmosphere which, especially nowadays, many of us crave. Growing a vertical garden indoors will help you feel like you're outdoors even when you can't go outside.

An Art Form

They offer an easy way to cover up bland, white walls. If you don't want to just hang up another painting on your wall, but you hate blank spaces, it's a creative and fun way to level up your space. A white wall can feel cold and uninviting, whether inside or outside. But, coming up with solutions to make it feel and look more welcoming isn't always straightforward. A living wall can quickly fix that for you.

Aside from covering a blank space, they are considered art. They're not so common that everyone will have seen them before, and they really make a statement. Imagine all the different textures and plants you can add, all the different shapes and sizes; it'll be something to look at and admire. Your guests will be talking about it for days.

For Privacy

If making a statement is not your goal, you may consider this an easy yet beautiful way to add privacy to your home. Unfortunately, as societies grow, we have less space; therefore, our neighbors are getting closer and closer to our private spaces. Sometimes, we need a little help to cover our balcony from the direct view of our neighbors, whether we live in apartments or stand-alone houses. Again, vertical gardens come to the rescue – they create a privacy screen, and because many plants thrive on them, they'll grow fast, making your space feel more secluded.

All in all, vertical gardens are trendy right now because people have made them so. We're always looking for what's next, what's new, and living walls are it at the moment. You can't scroll through social media without seeing several photos of millennials in front of living walls. So, they are trendy, but your main question might still be, why do I need one (or more) of those?

Read on.

Why Choose a Vertical Garden?

So far, we've covered health benefits, ecological benefits, and aesthetics. There is another advantage to vertical gardens, though, and that is practicality. If the reasons above aren't enough to convince you that this is something you need, then you might want to look at the practical reasons why a vertical garden would improve your life.

Vertical gardens can be more than decorative pieces; you can grow your own vegetables, fruits, herbs, and flowers on them as well. Without much effort, you'll have what you need from the farmer's market right on your doorstep – or maybe, your balcony. Besides being aesthetically pleasing, your vertical garden can also feed you, and again, you don't need a green thumb to make it happen.

When used for growing crops, the greatest thing about vertical gardens is that they're easy to both maintain and harvest. And you can grow a multitude of vegetables and herbs in a very small amount of space. If you have a big backyard, you might opt for a traditional garden, but the vertical garden is the way to go for those who do not have space. If you think your family and friends will love your new beautiful vertical wall, imagine telling them it also gives you the ingredients you need to make tasty family meals.

The question here shouldn't be, "Is this for me?" It should be, "Why hadn't I done this sooner?" Maybe you're being introduced to vertical gardens for the first time, or maybe you simply didn't know where to start. This is the book that will guide you and teach you everything you need to know about creating your very own vertical garden. This is the incentive you need to start now. Keep reading to find out more about vertical gardens and learn the answers to the questions that may have popped into your mind. Next, we're talking about how to choose the right place for your vertical garden.

Chapter 2: Where to Place Your Vertical Garden

In the previous chapter, we learned some things about vertical gardens, such as what they are and the benefits of creating your own. We also discussed the different dwellings that can make use of vertical gardens. In this chapter, we'll take a further look at where you should place your vertical garden. We'll consider areas that will benefit your plants and which plants are the best depending on specific conditions.

We have discussed various areas where a vertical garden or living wall would do very well due to its ecological and health benefits. Still, I promised you more, so here is a more detailed list of a few more areas and why these non-traditional gardens can add something valuable to them. Several case studies have been conducted to determine why and if vertical gardens work in these areas, and the results have been extremely promising. I'll mention some of those famous places below.

Vertical Gardens at Airports

Airports, much like hospitals, are one of those places that are aesthetically bland and lack color. They both serve specific purposes, and making their infrastructure look appealing is not one of their top priorities. Even though we can all understand this, airports worldwide have been stepping up their game by making smart and ecologically sound decisions that also add to their attractiveness and uniqueness. They've been incorporating living walls into their most bland, unimaginative spaces.

From boarding gates to the VIP lounges, some airports worldwide have added living walls to their spaces. Beyond their beauty, they also provide cleaner and safer air quality and help calm the travel-weary passengers. If you're ever in New Zealand or London, you can keep an eye out for them at Christchurch Airport or Heathrow Airport, respectively.

Bringing a piece of the outdoors inside is an incredibly effective method of making passengers want to spend more time at those locations, often choosing to fly predominantly from those airports and even spending larger amounts of time there before catching their flight. This usually translates to more money spent at duty-free shops, restaurants, and cafés. It's simple; if people are comfortable, they'll want to stay longer.

Vertical Gardens in Courtyards

I can't think of anything more relaxing or soothing than to spend an afternoon outdoors surrounded by nature. In busy cities, having a little bit of nature in your apartment complex or shared office courtyards acts as an incentive to enjoy the benefits of being outdoors. Aside from increasing your Vitamin D levels by dint of being outdoors, the calming effects of living walls can boost your mood and productivity.

Spending your lunch break near a living wall can give you what you need to continue your afternoon feeling more upbeat and positive, which helps you be more productive at work. Even a small living wall can improve courtyards, and people who frequent them would benefit from them tremendously.

Vertical Gardens in Rooftop Bars

I've told you all about the amazing benefits of having your own vertical garden right on your balcony, but rooftops are just as incredible at accommodating one or more of them. If the building you live in or where you work has a mostly-unused rooftop, why not turn it into a beautiful rooftop garden that everyone can enjoy? Moreover, as space is not an issue when dealing with vertical gardens, you won't be taking up any floor space, which means you can have a few benches or seats set out for everyone.

This trend has become popular among rooftop bars, where space is limited, and it helps create a sense of privacy from other nearby buildings. Plus, who doesn't enjoy drinking a cocktail in a chic environment that feels like you're in the middle of nature?

Vertical Gardens at Events

As more and more people are using out-of-the-box ideas to make their events unique, many have opted for living walls as their primary focus. Whether you are planning a birthday or an annual company party, a living wall will elevate the event while acting as a fabulous backdrop for photos, which can generate more interest in your event.

Some business events usually call for something different, exciting, and new because they have competitors trying to sell the same product or service. These types of events can gain the most from something as unique as a living wall. You can even customize the wall, choosing plants with colors and textures that suit your business' logo or vision.

Vertical Gardens Used for Branding

Aside from being a great way to make your business events unique, you can also consider using living walls for branding. If an eco-friendly approach is part of your business or products, sell it by making it known that you care about the environment. Creating sublime living walls is the easiest way to show off how forward-thinking your company is. It'll be a great addition to your building, and if you need any inspiration, the H&M headquarters in London has already done this. Brands like Nike, The Body Shop, and Volkswagen have adopted this branding technique as well.

Vertical Gardens in Public Spaces

Some cities have been utilizing living walls to make public spaces feel more welcoming. Places like train stations, car parks, markets, and public buildings like the post office are more enjoyable when they don't look like big cement blocks. Making public spaces more unique makes inhabitants feel happier, which can entice them to live in that city or near those spaces. It's not every day you see a living wall adorning your local train station, so imagine the smile on your face when you do.

Vertical gardens are a must in large cities. Adding them to public spaces will improve the city's aesthetics and inhabitants' health.

Vertical Gardens in Restaurants and Bars

Restaurants and bars nowadays are not only about the food or drinks they serve. In our society, the vibe and feel of a place are a vital part of every customer's experience there. Going out to eat or for a drink has become more about the general experience rather than just about the food and drinks you get. People are chasing what's new and contemporary and want something exciting to look forward to. This is why many restaurants and bars are adding living walls to their designs.

Some places, such as the Facebook Office in Dublin and the Crystal Serenity Cruises offices in the United States of America, have incorporated living walls in their space to give their customers a new dining experience. When used in bars, a living wall can also mean storing and growing your own herbs for cocktails and drinks, adding a fun and practical level to your clients' experience.

Vertical Gardens at Universities and Schools

We've already covered some of the positive effects of living walls, such as the ones they have on our stress levels, productivity, and rational or logical thinking. Incorporating these works of art into universities or secondary schools can increase motivation and decrease depression in students, especially if the living walls are located near libraries or lecture halls.

Students can feel more relaxed throughout their exams and study periods and experience the sensation of being outside, which will be beneficial, especially when they have to spend hours on end studying indoors.

Choosing the optimal wall or location in your space is important when creating these living walls. It requires some thinking and planning to find the optimal location, but fear not! The place you've been thinking about might just be the perfect one if you have the right tools, plants, and knowledge. One of the most important things to consider is how to keep your plants alive, so let's discuss that.

Keeping Your Living Walls Alive

When thinking of plants, water is likely to be one of the first things to cross your mind, and rightly so; watering your living wall, just like your potted plants, is necessary. There are a few different ways you can go about this, and you should consider them carefully before deciding where you want your living wall to be and what types of plants or herbs you want to grow.

Depending on your chosen system, you will have more or less flexibility as to which plants you can grow. As technology advances, you can also find various systems to use, some of which are more affordable than others. The less work you will have to do daily equals a higher price tag on your watering system. You can take the simplest route and water your vertical garden yourself, manually, but this method can take up a lot of time and effort, so be prepared.

The next section of the book describes the most common systems. Each one has its advantages and disadvantages; it's up to you to consider which type of vertical garden you want and the amount of time you can dedicate to it, while also keeping in mind the cost and efficiency levels.

Drip Irrigation System

This system is most efficient for your living wall because it uses a hydroponic system connected to your plumbing. This can be a problem, though, if you don't have a water source near your balcony or driveway. On a positive note, one major advantage of drip irrigation systems is that they can recycle water, which makes them more sustainable than other systems. You can reuse water from an air-conditioning unit, a coffee machine, or even the water you use to wash your vegetables.

Drip irrigation systems entail higher start-up costs but require less labor, which makes them quite efficient.

Tank System

Tank systems use replaceable trays; the soiled water in the trays has to be changed often. Unfortunately, they are not allowed in hospitals or places with strict hygiene codes to follow because they require more water and soil. This soil may lead to the appearance of pests and diseases that are not compatible with these types of facilities. This is a drawback not found in the drip irrigation systems mentioned earlier.

Tank systems also require more maintenance, such as frequent soil changes to prevent fungus and mold. This can be a deal-breaker for busy beginners.

Whichever system you go for, you'll also need to know which types of plants you'd be able to grow as each one is different and will, therefore, need specific care and maintenance.

What Type of Plants Should You Choose?

The list is extensive and varied. Are you thinking about aesthetics, practicality, or the difficulty of maintenance? Depending on your available time, budget, and needs, you'll be faced with many choices that should be taken into consideration when creating your vertical garden.

Whether you go for plants, herbs, vegetables, or fruit, you need to keep in mind the exact location they'll be living in and if they'll be happy growing near each other. Let's say you choose plants that grow at very different rates; you'll find that your little ones might not even grow at all, as they'll be overshadowed by the bigger ones and not have as much access to light as they need. If you choose woodier plants, which are thicker and heavier, you won't get that beautiful garden flow since they do not fall delicately downwards. With lighter plants like flowers or vines, you'll get that cascading effect that looks bushier and more appealing to the eye.

Another point to consider when choosing the right plants is whether you want to grow any fruits or vegetables. Not every fruit or vegetable can be grown successfully in a vertical garden. Some smaller-sized fruits and vegetables will thrive in these conditions. Larger produce such as apples or pumpkins is just not cut out for vertical gardening.

You have a lot of thinking to do before starting your own vertical garden. In Chapter Six, you'll find a more detailed explanation of which plants to choose based on the different specifications and a glossary to help you make your choice.

Choosing the right plants is important. What's just as important is giving them the right amount of sunlight. Let's take a quick look at that.

Sunlight vs. Shade

As you already know, vertical gardens can easily grow indoors; they need not be outside to survive. Sunlight is always important, so even if your vertical garden will be inside your home, you must consider what type of natural light it'll be exposed to.

One of the best tips is to never choose a spot fully exposed to sunlight or fully shaded from it. This will give you more flexibility when deciding on which plants to grow. This is the next most important factor to consider aside from your watering system, which we've already discussed. Even if you have plants that don't require a lot of exposure to sunlight, they may still need to be watered often, so finding a balance that suits your lifestyle will lead to a more successful vertical garden.

If your preferred location is not always exposed to sunlight, consider buying modular containers so that you can move them around as needed. This is especially useful if a plant is not doing so well in its location, and you wish to move that specific one instead of the entire vertical garden.

Most plants will include information on their bag or tag regarding the exposure and water levels they need, so make sure you look at that and keep this information in mind when starting your vertical garden.

In the next chapter, we'll look at how to pick the right soil for your plants.

Chapter 3: Picking the Right Soil

We've talked about some basics of vertical gardening, and in this chapter, we're looking at another important part of all types of gardening: picking the right soil. When starting your vertical garden or living wall, you have to start right at the base, the soil, before getting to the pretty plants, bright flowers, and luscious greens.

When it comes to choosing your soil, there are two different approaches. The most common one is to know what plants, flowers, fruits, or vegetables you want to grow and then choose the right soil for them. The other approach is to first pick your soil depending on your budget and then find plants that are compatible with that soil type. The second method is less common, but it may be suitable for some people.

Let's find out what types of soil exist and what soils some plants prefer so that you can keep that in mind when choosing your own.

Soil Types

The different soil types for your vertical garden or living wall are the same ones used for any type of gardening in general; it's all just soil. But the plants you choose will determine the best soil type for your vertical garden.

The different basic types of soil are:
1. Sandy soil
2. Clay
3. Silt
4. Peat
5. Chalky soil
6. Loam

Sandy Soil:

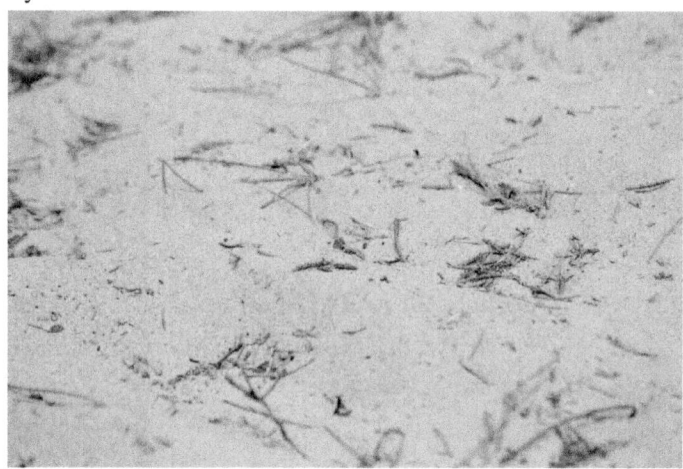

This type of soil is considered "light" soil; it has a high amount of sand and a low amount of clay, and sand is lighter than clay. It is also warm and dry and doesn't have many nutrients. Sandy soil can be easy to work with for a beginner, but it dries out in the summer, and the low amount of nutrients that it does have are easily washed away by water. It can be useful, though, if you're looking for a type of soil with quick water drainage.

Sandy soil can be improved with organic matter, which gives plants the nutrients they need. Growing herbs in this type of soil works well, so if you'd like to have your own herb garden with rosemary, salvia, or lavender, sandy soil might be the right soil for your vertical garden.

Clay:

Clay soil is on the opposite end of the spectrum from sandy soil. It contains high amounts of nutrients and is lumpy and sticky when wet but hard and smooth when dry, which makes it difficult to cultivate, especially if you're a beginner. Also, in contrast with sandy soil, clay soil is a slow-draining soil, so it keeps its nutrients, making it a good choice for plant growth.

This type of soil will definitely test your new skills and might not be the best choice for a vertical garden due to its weight; however, if you use it in a horizontal garden, sunflowers, cabbages, and broccoli thrive in clay soils.

Silt:

Silt is smooth to the touch and has a soapy consistency when it's moist. It is considered light soil but retains moisture better than sandy soil, so it has a higher amount of nutrients and is more fertile. Because its soil particles are medium-sized and fine, the soil structure is easily compacted. While it does retain its moisture, this means it retains the cold and drains poorly. It is nonetheless an easier soil to grow plants in than clay soil.

While not ideal for vertical gardening, lettuce and artichokes like silt, as do cabbages and even rice. The first two can be grown in a vertical garden; growing either or both of the second two entails special considerations.

Peat:

Peat soil is dark and soft to the touch. It has a high amount of organic matter but is low in nutrients. It retains water very well and may need extra care with drainage. The advantage of this is that it'll keep its moisture during the dry months, and even though this is not the type of soil you easily find in your garden, it is a great choice for planting.

Flowers love this soil, and ferns, camellias, and azaleas are the perfect match for peat soils.

Chalky Soil:

Chalky soils may not be the best for plant growth as they're alkaline (meaning they have a higher pH level), preventing many plants from growing in them. Ericaceous plants such as azaleas, camellias, hydrangeas, or some types of berries, hate chalky soil.

Because this soil is also free-draining, any minerals in it will be drawn away quickly by water, which means most plants will have a hard time growing. You can add fertilizers to this soil to make it more manageable for beginners. Some plants that do well in chalky soils are ivy, grapevines, and clematis.

Loam:

Loam is considered the best type of soil for growing plants. It's a mixture of silt, clay, and sand; it retains moisture well, but it also drains well - it's truly the perfect mix of soil. It has many nutrients due to the balance of the three types of soil, and it warms up easily in spring but doesn't dry out in summer like other types. For an easier time growing your vertical garden or living wall, loamy soil is the best to start with. You should always add organic matter or extra nutrients to it, but it is the easiest to manage.

As it's a gardener's best friend, loam can be used with most plants and flowers that don't require any of the specific characteristics of the other types of soil.

I've mentioned that different nutrients are needed by different plants, and you've probably been wondering what nutrients or organic matter are the most suitable for your plants. Let's have a look at that.

What Nutrients do Plants Need?

Simply put, plants need potassium, nitrogen, and phosphorus for growth. There are other important nutrients, such as calcium, sulfur, magnesium, and even metallic elements such as iron, manganese, zinc, and copper, but the first three are the main nutrients your plants are going to need to grow well.

Each nutrient has a different purpose, but the main three (called "NPK," after their designations on the periodic table) will give your plant healthier leaves and increase its longevity. If your plant's leaves are darker than normal and there's a loss of leaves, you might be looking at a phosphorus deficiency. If the upper leaves are light green and the lower ones are yellow and shriveled, then your plant probably lacks nitrogen. And if you see yellowing at the tips of your plant's leaves, it wants potassium.

As you can see, each nutrient contributes to a different aspect of a plant's health and appearance; making sure your soil has the right balance of nutrients will result in healthier, better-looking plants.

Adding Nutrients to Your Soil (Organically)

Now that you're aware of how important nutrients are for plant growth, let's talk about what you can do to add them to your soil organically. There are many ways to do this that won't break the bank.

- **Leaf Litter** – You can collect leaves around your garden or city area and use them to make compost or use them directly on your soil as mulch. When used this way, leaf litter will block weeds and increase moisture while slowly adding nutrients to your plant's soil.
- **Grass Clippings** – These are a great addition as they provide a lot of nitrogen to help keep leaves green and healthy. If you don't have a lawn of your own, you may be able to find collection points in your area where you can get them.
- **Compost** – It doesn't have to be difficult to make compost, and if you use it, your soil will use it all up. Use a mixture of grass clippings or weeds as your base, as they are high in nitrogen, with leaf litter or straw, as they are high in carbon. Those two nutrients combined will make the perfect addition to your soil.

- **Straw** – Even though this is a potentially expensive method of adding nutrients to your soil, it can be a good choice for those who have it.
- **Wood Chips** – This is a similar option to leaf litter in that it can be used as mulch. Wood chips decompose more slowly, so keep that in mind. They can also be added to your compost bin, as they are high in carbon.
- **Cover Crops** – Crops like vetch or clover are easily accessible, and they add nitrogen to the soil as they grow. Cover crops also work well because they attract pollinators.
- **Wood Ashes** – These add potassium to the soil, which prevents the yellowing of leaves. Wood ashes are especially great if you own a wood stove, as you'll already have them. Be careful if using them, as they can be a limiting agent. They're also less effective than commercially-bought lime if you're trying to raise the soil's pH levels.
- **Manure** – Manure is high in phosphorus, which will help with your plants' growth and health.

Starting by experimenting with any of these will teach you what's best for the soil you buy or use. It's not an exact science, as most soils vary from one area to another and from brand to brand, so don't worry too much; experimenting is part of owning a vertical garden or living wall, and if you ask me, it's the best part.

After deciding on the right type of soil and nutrients to add to it, you may be thinking, "But how much will I need?" This is a great question.

How Much Soil Do You Need?

You might just want to wing it and buy a few bags of potting soil and figure it out once you've started planting, but I wouldn't recommend that. You might end up with too much, or you might not have enough. Nobody wants to run to the garden center a second time to get more soil, especially when they're excited to start this journey into the world of vertical gardening and living walls. Thankfully, it's easy to find out how much soil you need before you start.

Whether you have a large or small container for your plants, the formula for soil volume in a rectangular or square-shaped container is easy to calculate. Start by measuring its length, width, and height in feet (or fractions of feet). The volume of the container is the product of multiplying those three measurements, which gives you a result in cubic feet. Once you get that number, divide it by 27 to get the exact number of cubic yards you need to buy.

Volume = Length x Width x Height (in feet)

Volume/27 = amount of soil to buy (in cubic yards)

If your container is not a rectangle or square, you may treat it as such to get the most approximate measurements. Err on the side of caution and round up, so that you have enough soil instead of having to go back to the store.

Preparation is key when taking up gardening; the more you know, the better you'll be able to handle problems when they arise. The same goes for preparing your vertical garden or living wall. There are different things to consider and prepare before you start planting. Let's look at a few of those things next.

Things to Consider When Preparing for a Vertical Garden

Besides everything else already mentioned, it's important to decide which structure you want to use to grow your vertical garden or living wall. You can buy containers or a freestanding structure, or even make your own.

If you decide to make your own vertical garden supporting structure, consider the materials from which you can build your structure. These structures can be made of wood, metal, plastic, iron, or a mixture of these materials. A very common structure utilizes an iron frame with wooden planks; this design is sturdy and is easily attached to a wall. If your vertical garden or living wall will be outdoors, consider weatherproofing treatments for both the wood and the metal.

You don't have to build this yourself; nowadays, it's easy to find ready-built or modular structures that suit the space and design concept you're going for. You can even go for a mix of both by buying a few parts and then DIY-ing the rest to adapt it to what you want.

Another factor to consider when preparing to build a vertical garden is to think about the wall or space where you want to place it. Preparing the wall to protect it against the roots of your plants is important, as well as preventing the humidity from the plants from getting into your wall. You'll have to water your plants, and you need to plan it so that you won't be watering your wall every day or every few days. If you're attaching your vertical structure to a wall, use a durable plastic sheet as a moisture barrier between the wall and the supporting structure.

Remember that different irrigation systems and options are available to you; when creating a living wall, having the right irrigation system is incredibly helpful and necessary to the well-being of your plants as well as the wall itself.

For example, if you really want an irrigation system, a drip system will be safer for the drywall and interior-grade paint behind your plants than a waterfall or heavy misting or sprinklers.

It's all about balance, and you can do it if you think of everything ahead of time. To help you make the best decisions, in the next chapter, we'll be talking about the pros and cons of containers, planters, and trellises.

Chapter 4: Containers, Planters, and Trellises

You're almost ready! You have thought about the ideal space for your vertical garden and its level of exposure to sunlight, as well as the right soil for the plants you want to grow. This chapter will help you to decide if you want to use containers, planters, or trellises in your vertical structure.

We'll be looking at the differences between the three options available to you, as well as some exciting, cheap DIYs you can use to add that extra touch your space is lacking.

There are three main options, with subdivisions to consider, so let's find the right one for you.

Containers

Containers can be made of the most imaginative materials as well as the more common ones. Pots are the most commonly used container by gardeners; they're versatile, cheap if made from plastic, and are what most people use in their homes. You can buy them at garden centers and supermarkets, and you can find a wide variety of sizes that suit your needs. I especially love clay pots; I find them pleasing to the eye, and they are a good option for a vertical herb garden. They can be a little heavy, so the structure you use to hang them must be solid.

You can have fun with containers by thinking outside of the box. Even if pots can be relatively cheap, you may want to be more environmentally friendly and recycle some everyday products like plastic bottles or tin cans. By reusing these items, you won't be adding any extra costs to your vertical garden, and they work as well, or better than store-bought standard fare. They are usually lighter than clay or ceramic vases, so this is a good option if you're not very confident about the strength or durability of your vertical structure.

You can even reuse glass jars, which would look beautiful with different shapes, sizes, and colors hanging on a wall. Just remember openings for drainage; glass weep-holes would have to be drilled, not cut or punched out. A trend that has appeared recently is glass terrariums filled with succulents that look great while maintaining moisture levels in the terrarium.

An easy way to create your own containers which are still chic is to use landscape fabric to create little pockets. You then fill these pockets with your soil and seeds, and then you can simply hang them on any wall. I love how simple, easy, cheap, yet strikingly elegant this looks in or outside a home.

Planters

Planters are typically made of wood, and they can have standard garden beds or raised garden beds. Vertical planters can also include the use of rope, hooks, pipes, and wire.

Your creativity can take charge here as you'll decide how to create your vertical planter. You can go for a geometrical feel or a cleaner, industrial vibe. You can also mix and match plants and flowers or add different herbs. You can hang planters from the ceiling, but they can also be attached to a wall using plywood or pipes. Rope is also a commonly used material, and if you are bothered by the appearance of traditional rope, you can find different colors and match them to your plants or containers.

The sky is truly the limit when it comes to your preferences and style. Planters are great because they're effortlessly stunning, whereas, with a tin, plastic, or clay container, you might need to do a little more to it if you're going for a specific look. Moreover, because you have so much freedom over your planter's style, you can easily adapt the materials you use to fit them into your budget. You can even use things you have lying around your home, transforming them into chic

or beautiful planters that will hold your favorite plants.

Trellises

A trellis is a latticework structure usually made from wood, metal, or even bamboo. It is mainly used for plants but can have other uses too. Plants wrap and anchor themselves onto the trellis - sometimes with a little help from us gardeners, which we do by tying them to its framework when they're growing. These architectural structures are beautiful in and of themselves, so even when your plants are just seeds or little sprouts, your vertical garden or living wall will already be looking fantastic.

Another benefit of trellises is that they are very easy to install. They can be used just as a structure of their own to complement garden beds. A trellis can be attached to a wall, too, for a simple way to allow your plants to grow vertically. This is a great option for a living wall to create a privacy screen, as discussed earlier. This will provide you with more intimacy, even when your plants are not fully grown, as the trellis pattern will help conceal your space slightly.

Because a trellis makes your plants interwoven and close together when they've grown, it creates a barrier for noise and wind, and the trellis itself is usually easy to clean. The problems arise when bad weather damages the trellis. Even when they are made of metal, being placed outdoors makes them susceptible to corrosion or rust. This means you'll either have to buy a new one from time to time or apply specific treatments to protect the one you own.

Moreover, if they're exposed to extreme weather conditions, they have the tendency to shrink or bend. A wooden trellis may also grow mold and mildew if not treated properly. These disadvantages may lead to higher costs in maintaining the structure itself, but a trellis is still easy to set up and looks great from day one.

The table below gives you a summary of the pros and cons mentioned for each type of structure. It will hopefully allow for easier comparison between them and help you choose which one to use.

	Containers	**Planters**	**Trellis**
Pros	+ Easily moved for better light or shade + Virtually no weed problems + Less risk of soil-borne disease	+ Aesthetically pleasing + Mix and match different plants and succulents + Simple upkeep	+ Stunning from day one + Easy to clean + Perfect for creating privacy in an open or high visibility area

| Cons | - A lot of different containers to water if you don't use an irrigation system
- Less attractive when just starting out
- More preparation required | - Require some creativity
- More preparation required
- Harder to move as a single unit | - Potential higher cost to maintain
- Exposure to the elements leads to structural damages
- Mold and mildew may occur |

DIYs: Making your Own Containers, Planters, and Trellises

Wire Wall Planter

All you'll need for this DIY project is wire or steel mesh, pots, rings, and hooks. It's that simple!

Wire or steel mesh is a material you can get at most any garden or hardware store. There is a wide variety of sizes, colors, and patterns. This part is fun as you can choose a common trellis shape, a crisscross or lozenge shape, or go for something totally different like simple squares. It's up to you!

The pots you choose can be made of clay, plastic, or ceramic. Because you'll be attaching the wire mesh to a wall, the structure will be solid enough for heavier pots. Make sure your pots have a hole at the bottom for draining water. Keep in mind that because they'll be hanging, you won't be able to add a pot tray underneath them.

The hooks will connect your pots to the wire mesh.

Follow the instructions below to make this quick and easy **DIY** wire wall planter:

1. Place the wire mesh against the wall and drill a few holes just below the top edge of the wireframe. The heavier the pots, the more holes and hooks you'll need to ensure it's durable.
2. Add wall plugs to the drilled holes for a more stable structure.
3. Once done, screw hooks into the wall plugs. The hooks will support the wire mesh.
4. After that, hang your wire mesh. Make sure it's level and tightened to your liking.
5. Hang the pots using hooks and rings to go around each pot.
6. Voilà! Your vertical wall is ready!

To make your planter more unique and eye-catching, paint the wall behind it or even add some colorful rope along the wire – but be sure to do this before your plants are fully grown. You can also add a garden bed below the planter (if it's outdoors) and grow climbing plants that will use the wire mesh as their support – a simple and beautiful idea to **DIY** your first vertical garden.

Recycled Bottles

Going with a simpler and cheaper method, recycled bottles are easy to use and very accessible. You won't need many materials, and this **DIY** project can be done in just under an hour or so, depending on how large you want this project to be.

The materials you'll need for this are very straightforward:

- Plastic bottles, empty and clean
- Scissors
- Thread, wire, or rope

Follow the instructions below to make this easy, environmentally friendly DIY planter:

1. After cleaning your plastic bottles thoroughly, cut a large, rectangular hole on one side of your bottle. This is where your seedlings will go and where your plants will grow out of.

2. Then, make two tiny holes on each side of the rectangle you just cut out. These four tiny holes will be used to pass your thread, wire, or rope to ensure your container is well secured.

3. Once you've passed the cordage through the two left and two right holes, tie a large knot to hold the bottle in place. Decide what spacing you want between each bottle, then repeat.

4. Last, make two or three weep-holes at the bottom of the container to permit drainage.

5. Hang it all on a wall using strong hooks, or nail it, and you're done!

This incredibly simple DIY project means that you can start this today, right now. We all have a few extra bottles lying around the house, and this is the project to use them in!

Shoe Organizer Vertical Garden

As strange as this DIY project may sound, it actually works very well and is a simple way to create a vegetable or herb garden in your kitchen or on your balcony. This is a list of what you'll need for this project:

- A hanging shoe organizer (which has several pockets)
- A pole or pipe with its respective attachments
- Strong hanging hooks
- Wood plank (optional)
- A tray or garden bed (optional)

You can hang this shoe organizer garden wherever you want. Depending on the weight it must support and the wall material to which you'll be screwing it, use the right tools and anchors so that your vertical structure is sturdy. Follow the instructions below to do this creative DIY project:

1. Attach the pole or pipe (a curtain pole, for example) to the wall.

2. Use the strong hooks to hold the shoe organizer and connect it to the pole or pipe you've mounted. Remember that even if the storage pouch may be light, with the added soil, plants, and water, it will get heavy. The hooks need to support all that total weight.

3. Then, to check drainage, pour water into each pocket. If there's no visible drainage, make a few holes in them.

4. Once it's all done, add your soil and plants, and it's ready.

5. An optional step is to push the vertical garden away from a wall by drilling or gluing a wood plank onto the wall behind the structure. For a more environmentally friendly option, use a pot tray or even a garden bed below your structure so that the excess water from the pockets drains into it. This means that less water will be wasted as it will water the plants below.

Who would have known that such a simple product like a shoe organizer could have such a fun purpose as well?

Pallet Planter

This DIY is the easiest and cheapest one yet. All you need is a pallet (or two, or more depending on the size of your vertical garden) and a few containers of your choice. You won't have to change the pallet at all, but you should paint or weatherproof it if attaching it to a wall or solid structure outside.

You'll use the bottom side of the pallet as it has spaces between the wood slats, and these will act as shelves. If you can get them, euro pallets are the best for this DIY project as they come with three shelves, and each shelf has two rectangular openings that will accommodate one container. If you have difficulty finding the right sized container for the openings, tack a wood slat over the shelf opening to reduce its size to something closer to that of the container.

This DIY project will be a great start for your vertical garden. It can help you test the waters and get the hang of things before moving onto something bigger and more costly.

Whether you buy or make your vertical garden or living wall structure, you'll have the means to grow your own plants, vegetables, fruit, or flowers. With the knowledge in this chapter, you'll be better prepared to make an informed decision when it comes to how much or how little effort you want to put into your vertical garden project before you get started. One thing I'm sure of is that you should have some fun while doing it and also that you're more than capable of doing one or all of these DIY projects!

Starting your vertical garden or living wall need not be a daunting task. You can do it right now. Using the information in this book, and a little effort and passion, in just a few weeks, you can be drinking your morning coffee or tea, looking at your new green wall, and wondering how you could have ever lived without it for so long.

In the next chapter, we'll revisit a few points and summarize a list of things you need to start your vertical garden.

Chapter 5: The Vertical Gardening Start-Up

By now, you're probably feeling excited and confident about starting your new hobby, gardening. You're feeling even more thrilled about covering up that ugly, blank wall you've had in your home for far too long. You're ready to get your hands dirty - literally, as they'll be covered in soil - and you can't wait to get started. So, to make sure you're ready, we will go through all the different steps and things you need to get everything up and running.

This will be a recap and summary of everything you need to think about and decide on in order to have a successful start. Use this chapter as a guide through the different options and ideas available to you. It will help you find the best options for your situation and serve as a reminder that you're in charge, and your creativity will lead you wherever you allow it to.

Use this as a checklist (as well as the real checklist at the end of the chapter) to get started. Tick off things as you go, and you'll be a step closer to getting this done right. Let's go through these options and steps together.

Installing Your First Vertical Garden

Choose Your Wall/Spot

This should go without saying, but here I am, saying it. Before any plans are made, or any DIY projects are started, you need to know exactly where you want your vertical garden to go. Consider the spot for its purpose. Is it a sunny wall that happens to get too hot early in the afternoon, and you need a way to cool it down? Is it a way to get some privacy from neighbors directly across from you? Or is it a sustainable way to grow some of your own produce?

The purpose of this garden will dictate which wall or spot you choose, so think about it carefully. Once you have decided on it, consider the different ways you can hang or place a vertical garden in that space. Will it be okay for you to drill into it? Is it a strong enough wall to have heavy containers hanging off of it? If you're renting, do you have permission to do so? If your spot is indoors, think about potential humidity issues since you don't want to damage any furniture or walls with your newfound passion.

Once your spot is chosen and you're sure you can make it happen there, you'll be able to choose your type of containers, trellis, and even plants because you'll know what the conditions of that spot are.

What Plants Are You Going to Choose?

The next step is a fun one! Plants, vegetables, herbs, flowers, or fruit? You now get to choose what you want to grow and see in your vertical garden. You can choose by color or size, and if going for herbs, you can even grow new ones to test them in your favorite dishes.

Since you already know the location of your vertical garden, you'll get to make an informed decision on what plants or produce are the best to plant. This is the easiest way to create your first vertical garden as you don't find yourself needing to move it around later on. Sometimes, moving it around isn't even an option as your garden might be too heavy, or you just don't have space anywhere else. Choosing what plants you can grow in the chosen spot is the way to ensure a successful start.

To learn more about plants and which ones are the best choice for you, read Chapter 6, where you'll find a detailed list of the best plants for your vertical garden and living wall. This includes information about soil, watering, and how to plant them.

The Right Soil for Your Plants

Knowing which plants you want to grow will make the choice of soil easy. This is because each plant requires a specific type of soil with more or fewer nutrients, more or fewer fertilizers, and even more or less water.

This decision should be made after picking which plants or flowers you prefer. This will give you a wider variety of colors and plant types to choose from for the vertical garden of your dreams. However, if you don't want to bother with different soil types because of specific plant requirements, you can choose plants that all need the same type of soil. This may limit your options in plant selection, but it may also help you as a beginner not to get mixed up.

Whichever path you'll take, this is a decision you cannot skip as the soil is the base, the home for your plants, and it will directly impact how well they will grow and flourish.

To Fertilize or Not to Fertilize

If you have some doubts on whether to use fertilizers or not, you may check Chapter 3, where we discussed it thoroughly. Helping your soil by adding necessary nutrients to it may determine the successful growth of your plants. Even if the soil you choose is the right one for a plant, it doesn't mean it has everything it needs to flourish. Nutrients will give it that extra boost, especially when it's still a sprout.

When drainage is not an issue, your type of soil might allow water to wash away many of its nutrients; therefore, your plant will not thrive. You may not be at fault – soils all have a different percentage of nutrients; even identical bags of store-bought potting soil are all slightly different in this regard. So, adding some nutrients will help prevent that nutrient loss or just give your plants a boost they'll be happy to get.

You can go fully organic and environmentally friendly by reusing materials available to you, or you can get them store-bought. Choosing to fertilize shouldn't be a question, and the options for fertilizer are endless – just re-read Chapter 3 for some ideas on how to fertilize your plants.

Where to Grow: Containers or Trellis

The next step on your checklist should be to decide whether you prefer containers, planters, or a trellis. Any of these is an amazing option. There isn't one better than the others in general, but there should be a clear winner to you, depending on the space you have and where you'll place your vertical garden.

If your vertical garden is on your very small balcony, I'd say a trellis is probably the way to go. It will take up a tiny bit of floor space. If you use containers, there is a chance they will take up a bit more volume. One way around this is to hang them, in which case you can keep your floor space free for other things.

You may also be thinking about the aesthetics. Do you want a freestanding trellis to decorate a patio? Do you prefer a modern approach, using concrete containers that contrast with the green of the plants? Maybe you're even considering both: a couple of raised garden beds underneath a trellis attached to a wall.

Now that you know your chosen spot well and the type of plants you want to grow, making this decision should be easier. Just remember that it's your space, and you're the one who needs to love it. Whether convenience, beauty, or practicality, you're in charge.

Don't Forget the Gardening Tools

We haven't talked about them yet, so you'll be pleased to know that you don't have to buy a huge supply of gardening tools, nor do you need to buy any top-of-the-line ones. Start with the basics, and as you go along, you'll get more or better tools that will help make your job easier.

For a first-time vertical gardener, I would get the following gardening tools: gardening gloves, gardening fork, garden trowel, shears, pruners, scissors, and a watering can (a hose will work fine if you're outside). If you feel like spending time working in your garden is something you will often do and don't have old clothes, invest in an apron.

These tools will help you maneuver the soil, move things around, and water your plants (if you choose not to have an automatic irrigation system). They will also help you take care of your vertical garden in the long run, as you'll need to prune certain plants from time to time. You need not get the most expensive tools to start; a cheap, plastic version will do just fine at first.

Should You Decorate Your Vertical Garden?

This is an added step that is entirely optional. It's if you want to go the extra mile and jazz up your vertical garden or living wall a little more. You can do different things to make it even more interesting to look at. Sometimes just the way you place your containers will create a stunning, eye-catching piece of décor.

You can do a little or a lot with your space, and decorating it might just help give it that extra touch of beauty. For example, if you decide to use the recycled bottles project discussed in chapter four, you may want to paint them a unique color. Pink or black will contrast well with the green of the plants. If you have colorful flowers planted in your living wall, then you can also tie them together with a background color.

You could also add lights above your vertical garden or living wall to make it stand out even more. Colored LEDs are also very trendy right now and can be easily placed around your living wall. You could also hang a long container high up on your wall and let the plants or flowers flow downwards at different levels to create a magical look. You could even go as far as using ornate frames around your containers to make them stand out even more.

Your decorations don't have to be too complicated, though. Something as simple as adding small stones or pebbles at the bottom of clear containers will create a modern and chic look, with the added benefit of helping your soil's drainage. You can also think outside of the box, literally, and extend the style you currently have inside your home into your vertical garden. It'll be worth it.

Watering Your Plants: Manually, Automatic Irrigation, or a Mix of Both?

You'll have to consider this step carefully before going ahead with the project because it can impact your budget. Moreover, it may also alter what type of structure you want to get if you choose an irrigation system that is better applied to a specific type of vertical structure. Don't worry though, since you're planning ahead, you still have some flexibility. You'll have the opportunity to adapt and change your mind before you set out on this task.

When considering how to water your plants, you should think about how much time you'd like to spend taking care of your plants. There will always be routine maintenance, but watering plants can be done easily without the need for a watering can.

Utilizing an irrigation system gives you the freedom to spend less time taking care of your plants. There are a few different irrigation systems, from simple to more complex models, cheaper to more expensive, etc.

There's a gravity-fed drip irrigation system. This involves a traditional drip irrigation system using a tank or water container at the top of your garden, which simply lets gravity do its work. If you have a tiered layer system, the drip method only needs to drip water onto the top containers. The water from those will subsequently drip onto the next ones until the extra water falls into a draining tray.

If you want a more complex system because your plants need regular watering, you might consider adding watering pipes on every row of your vertical garden. This involves a higher functioning system where you'll be sure that every plant gets the amount of water it needs. You can even install a timer to control when and for how long water is released, making the system more precise when watering your vertical garden.

You can also use a mixture of both types of systems where you manually deliver water to the top row of your plants while they'll drain the water onto the next row and so on. This involves more time and work on your part, but it's easier than having to water every single one of your containers, especially when you have a very large vertical garden.

Let's look at a simple DIY drip irrigation system that you can install in your vertical garden.

DIYing a Drip Irrigation System

To make your very own gravity drip irrigation system, make sure you have the following supplies:

- A water tank
- Malleable pipes, such as a hose or water distribution pipes, with only one end open
- Water emitters
- A timer

The water tank should be installed above your vertical garden, as this drip irrigation system uses gravity to function. The pipes, which must be malleable enough to bend from row to row, will be connected to the opening of the water tank and placed on the soil of each container. Once you've found the right place and secured the pipe as needed, you'll attach the water emitters to where you want your plants to be watered. You can add as many as you want, and these usually have a pressure fit system to make it easier for you to insert them. You can also adjust the amount of water that is delivered through the water emitters. This is done by using a timer to water your plants a specific amount at regular intervals instead of having them running continuously.

As promised, here is your start-up vertical gardening checklist:
- Wall or spot
- Your favorite plants
- Right soil for your plants
- The most suitable fertilizer for you
- Containers or Trellis
- Gardening tools
- Decoration (optional)
- Watering method

If you've ticked all of the boxes above, congratulations! You're ready to start your journey into vertical gardening and living walls. In the next few chapters, we'll dive into the best plants, fruits, veggies, and flowers for your vertical structure. They will give you all the information you need to choose the best ones for you and your space. Be sure to read those before you go off to buy your first plants.

Chapter 6: Best Plants for Your Vertical Garden

Getting the best plants for your vertical garden requires a few steps. You should choose the ones you love, and if we're talking about herbs, the ones you currently use in your dishes. An herb may be fun to plant, but it'll just take up space if you don't use it. That said, because we're dealing with a vertical garden, it's better to choose plants on the smaller side with minimal root systems. These plants won't need as much soil, so everything is lighter when hung up on your structure.

Another question you have to consider is what type of herbs or plants grow well together. Will you grow them in the same container, or should you separate some of them for optimal growth? Sunlight and water are also things you need to think about. If an herb needs more light, it should be placed on the top row. However, if that herb needs more water, it should go at the bottom to collect the most water if you're using a layered row system.

You'll also need to remember to replace certain herbs every year (or more often in some cases) if they seem overgrown. If they are overgrown, the roots will fill up their container, which stresses those plants. Therefore, it's better to keep them on rotation by having extra containers and swapping them as needed. This way, you'll have a beautiful vertical garden all year round.

But let's take a look at what herbs you should include in your vertical garden and which ones may be the best for you.

In the glossary below, you'll find the best herbs for your vertical garden:

1. Basil
2. Chives
3. Cilantro
4. Dill
5. Lavender
6. Marjoram
7. Mint
8. Oregano
9. Parsley
10. Rosemary
11. Sage
12. Tarragon
13. Thyme

Basil

Who doesn't love pesto? And if you don't, there are many other ways to use basil in your cooking. This herb is an incredibly fragrant one that loves full sun and grows well alongside tomatoes. In just a few weeks, you'll be able to harvest your first leaves, which is something you should do regularly to keep it going strong.

To plant basil, you can start with the seedlings inside your home, where it's warmer. You can do this for up to six weeks before the temperature rises. Basil likes its soil to be warmer than 50°F, so plan well, and don't forget that temperatures tend to drop at night. Basil should get 6 to 8 hours of full sun daily to grow well. To make sure it gets enough sunlight, this can be one of the plants you keep on your top rows.

- Plant the seeds about a quarter of an inch into the soil, spaced 10 to 12 inches apart.
- The soil should be moist, as basil loves moisture. This is why a vertical garden is great for this plant because it allows greater drainage. Basil prefers moist but well-drained soil.
- Once you see a few leaves, prune to above the second set to encourage more branches to grow. Repeat this every time, pruning it back to its first set of leaves.

Chives

Chives bloom in the summer with the most amazing colors, and they're a great addition to dips or sauces. However, be careful when planting them as they are an invasive type of plant and will take over other ones. If you're using a shoe organizer or pocket system, you won't have this issue. They love cooler temperatures, so you can plant them in the fall or spring as long as the temperature of the soil is around 65° F. They take their time to germinate, so don't be worried if you don't get results in the first couple of weeks. They need full sun, but they may also do okay in light shade. Their soil needs to be moist, well-draining, and very rich in nutrients, so incorporate fertilizers freely.

- Plant the seeds about a quarter of an inch into the soil, spaced 2 inches apart.
- Keep the soil thoroughly moist, and if you can see their bulbs (they grow near the surface), cover them with mulch to keep them moist too.
- The flower's seeds spread easily, so if you want to limit your planting area, remove their flowers once they bloom.

Cilantro or Coriander

You may have heard of this plant being referred to as cilantro, or maybe you heard people calling it coriander... the fact is they're the same! Cilantro refers to the plant's leaves used as an herb, and coriander refers to the seeds used as a spice.

Either you love cilantro, or you hate it. Many people say it tastes like soap to them. This is believed to be caused by aldehyde in soaps, which is found naturally in cilantro. However, if you do love it, this plant is a great choice for your vertical garden! It is fast-growing, aromatic, and prefers cooler temperatures, just like chives.

This plant loves light but shouldn't be grown during high temperatures as it will bolt (meaning it produces a flowering stem before harvest and the leaves are usually bitter and not good for consumption). You can place this plant in a spot in your vertical garden that gets enough light during the day but is also shaded.

- Plant the seeds about a quarter of an inch into the soil, spaced 1 to 2 inches apart.
- Keep the seeds moist during their germination and sow them every three weeks.
- Once the plant is established, it won't require as much water, so be careful not to overwater it.

Dill

Dill might not be in everyone's pantries, but it's a great addition to soups and stews and is used in pickling. It is an easy plant to grow. It likes soil temperature to be around 65° F. Once planted, seedlings should appear quickly, in just under two weeks. If you want a constant supply of dill, you may plant it every couple of weeks or allow it to flower and bolt so that its seeds spread, and you'll have more the following year.

- Plant the seeds about a quarter of an inch into the soil, spaced 18 inches apart.
- Place its container in full sun with well-draining soil that is rich in organic matter.
- When you start seeing seedlings, thin the plants to about 15 inches apart if they aren't already like that.
- Keep the soil moist and water it abundantly when growing the plant.

Lavender

Lavender is one of the most versatile plants and is used for eating, cleaning, or décor. It has the most beautiful scent and will look beautiful any time of the year in your home. Another benefit is that it attracts butterflies and bees, which will help pollinate your garden.

Even though this plant has amazing benefits, not only for your garden but in your home as well, it may not be the easiest to plant, so you should consider buying starter plants instead of seeds. They are an easy plant when it comes to soil, as they thrive in most soil types, even a dense one like clay. Just make sure you add organic matter if you intend to use a compacted soil to improve drainage, as lavender doesn't like a lot of moisture. In fact, its roots will rot easily if there is excess moisture, so be careful even when watering them.

- Plant it two to three feet apart.
- Use mulch to keep weeds away but be careful with the excess moisture mulch can bring to the plant's crown, as it'll create root rot.
- Water it once or twice a week until the plant is established, and then only every two to three weeks. Once you see its buds formed, go back to watering it once or twice a week.
- If you live in a region that experiences severe cold during winter, consider moving the plants indoors where it has a lot of light but is protected from the harsh weather. A modular system would be great for this plant.

Marjoram

You can use marjoram in most of your dishes as a seasoning. It also works great in any meat dish. It has a very mild flavor, so don't be afraid to test it out. This plant likes light and well-draining soil. If you want it ready for spring, you can start its growth indoors in early spring or late winter. Soak the seeds overnight and then sow them into potting soil. Once they are established, you can transplant the seedlings outside when the temperatures rise.

- Plant the seeds about 12 inches apart.
- Water them regularly, making sure to add nutrients to them occasionally to maximize growth.
- To generate new growth, prune it to close to the soil. Do this once flower buds appear, indicating the end of the harvesting period.

Mint

Who doesn't love mint? It's favored by many people because this plant smells incredible and makes a great herb for many dishes and even cocktails. Growing it is easy. Some may even say too easy, as it will completely take over your other plants. Planting mint is great, but you should isolate it from other plants.

This plant loves light, well-drained soil and will tolerate some shade. You can plant mint near tomatoes, but not in the same container because they take over the tomato plant. In colder temperatures, either bring the container inside or cover it to protect the plant.

- Plant them 2 feet apart.
- Keep the soil moist but use a light mulch to keep the leaves clean.

- Prune them generously and often. If they are controlled in a container, you shouldn't have an issue. Be aware that they are easily pulled out since they are shallow-rooted.

Oregano

You cannot think of Italy or pizza without thinking of oregano; one does not exist without the other. This plant is very versatile as an herb, and it's an excellent ground cover, even when using it in your vertical garden. You'll want to keep it somewhere sunny and only plant it when the temperature rises. Like the other plants, you can plant it indoors and then transfer it outside when it gets warmer.

This plant is not difficult to grow, so you can plant seeds or use a cutting from an established plant. You can grow it in the same container as any other vegetable, as oregano is a good companion plant and won't take over others.

- Plant the seeds 8 to 10 inches apart.
- Use well-draining soil and water it thoroughly but less often – touch the soil to see if it's dry; only water it if it is.
- Trim it regularly to increase growth and branching.
- You can harvest the leaves as you need them, but the most flavorful ones are found right before the flowers bloom.

Parsley

Parsley is from the same family as dill, but possibly a lot more common in our kitchens. This herb goes well with fewer dishes as it can have a strong flavor, but it will pair beautifully with plain white rice. One of its biggest advantages is that it's rich in iron and vitamins A and C, so use it abundantly in your cooking.

This plant loves the sun and needs to get about six to eight hours of it every day. A nutrient-rich and well-draining soil is the best for parsley. You'll know it's ready to harvest when the leaf stems have three segments. Always cut the outer leaves, and the inner ones will continue to mature. To speed up its growth, you may want to start planting it indoors about eight weeks before the last spring frost. You can then move them outside about four weeks later.

- Plant the seeds about a quarter of an inch into the soil, spaced 6 to 8 inches apart.
- Keep the soil moist at all times while the seeds germinate – it will take some time for you to see seedlings, but be patient; they will appear.
- If the temperature gets too high, water it abundantly and add mulch to help keep the soil moist.

Rosemary

Rosemary is such a beautiful herb to keep in your pantry; it adds flavor to your lamb, stews, and any type of grilled fish. You can do so much with a simple branch, and if you grow it in your vertical garden, it will likely remain green all year round. This is an easy plant to grow.

However, it may be difficult to grow from seed, so, if you can, buy a starter plant to put into one of your containers.

This plant loves the sun, well-draining soil, and space. Trim it often, as rosemary can spread about four feet in all directions, so keeping it contained is important for your vertical garden. Don't over-water it, as rosemary does not like to be consistently wet.

- Sow the seeds or starter plant in well-draining soil. If the temperatures are lower than 70° F, consider bringing your container indoors or plant it later in the year when the temperatures have risen.
- Water it regularly but be careful not to overwater it – this plant does not like being wet. If your vertical garden is layered, consider placing it in the top row.

- When grown, you can cut off the stems and dry them in your kitchen by hanging them.

Sage

According to some myths, if you want to do well in business, you need to grow sage in your garden. If you don't use this herb in the kitchen often, that may be a good reason for growing it. This plant blooms the prettiest flowers in different colors and if you want the edible variety, consider planting the variety called Salvia officinalis, as this is the one most commonly used in the kitchen.

Sage likes full sun exposure and well-draining soil. It doesn't like being overwatered when it's established, just like rosemary, so be careful not to water it if the soil is still moist. Also, like rosemary, it is easier to grow from a starter plant.

- Plant the seeds 2 feet apart in well-drained soil. You can sow them two weeks before the last spring frost for a head start.
- Water the plant regularly while it's still growing to avoid it drying out. Once established, check the soil moisture before watering it.
- Prune it every year for a more active plant and replace it every few years.

Tarragon

Tarragon, especially French tarragon, is a great herb to pair with meats and seafood. It's a beautiful green plant with a lot of texture that will look great in your vertical garden. Tarragon must be planted as a cutting from an established plant, which you can then transplant into your own vertical garden.

- Plant the established plants two feet apart in well-drained soil.
- Water them regularly and use mulch if the temperature is very low during fall and winter.
- Prune them often to avoid flowering.

Thyme

Thyme is such a fun plant. It's unique-looking and adds a beautiful, new shade of green to any vertical garden. Its usage in the kitchen is well known, and it can even help you get rid of insects!

Even though this plant is versatile and tastes delicious in most recipes, it does not grow very well from seeds. This means you're better off buying a starter plant for your vertical garden. It loves full sun exposure and heat and does not like to be wet, like rosemary. So be careful not to overwater it.

- Plant your young plant when the temperature is above 70° F.
- Make sure the soil is draining well so that your plant is not wet at all times, and only water it again when the soil is fully dry.
- Grow it near rosemary as they have similar needs.
- Prune it once or twice a year to contain its growth.

The table below shows you the different types of plants discussed and a summary of their properties:

Herb	Sun Exposure	Soil Type	Soil pH	Bloom
Basil	Full sun	Loamy	Slightly Acidic to Neutral	Summer
Chives	Full sun	Loamy, sandy	Slightly Acidic to Neutral	Summer
Cilantro	Full sun, Part sun	Loamy	Neutral	Spring
Dill	Full sun	Loamy, sandy	Slightly Acidic to Neutral	Summer
Lavender	Full sun		Neutral to Alkaline	Summer
Marjoram	Full sun	Loamy	Neutral	
Mint	Full sun	Loamy	Neutral	
Oregano	Full sun	Loamy	Neutral	Summer
Parsley	Full sun, Part sun	Loamy, sandy	Slightly Acidic to Neutral	
Rosemary	Full sun	Loamy, sandy	Slightly Acidic to Neutral	Summer
Sage	Full sun	Loamy, sandy	Slightly Acidic to Neutral	Summer
Tarragon	Full sun, Part sun	Loamy, sandy	Slightly Acidic to Neutral	
Thyme	Full sun, Part sun	Loamy, sandy	Alkaline	

For the best results, consult the table above and match herbs that work well together and require similar care or have similar growth patterns. This will make it easier for you as a beginner; however, if you truly love a variety of different plants, go ahead. Plant it, anyway! Remember my first tip; you have to love them. It's your vertical garden and your decision, so just have fun doing it.

The Best Plants for Living Walls

Now that we've covered the best herbs for your living wall, let's look at which non-edible plants are suitable for your space. Maybe you're thinking about what plants work best indoors. Perhaps you live in a windy city, so you need stronger stalks and stems. These are all important considerations when putting together your living wall. In this next section, we will be looking at the best non-edible plants for your living wall.

We'll talk about foliage plants that tolerate darker spots and others that do well in drier soil. We have it all – this is a list that will help you choose the best plants for your space. You may have a lot of sunlight but not a lot of time to water your plants, or more time but not as much light. It's all possible if you plan ahead carefully. Let's look at your options.

In the glossary below, you'll find the best plants for your living wall:

1. Air plants
2. Coleus
3. Croton
4. Elephant Ears
5. English Ivy
6. Hosta
7. Pothos
8. Spider plants

Air plas

This type of plant is part of the bromeliad family and is easily grown without soil. This means it can be a great plant to include in your hydroponic irrigation system if you're installing one. They love light and water but don't do so well if they cannot dry off, so if you're planting them in your living wall, make sure your container and irrigation system is set to let them dry after watering. Good air circulation is important for them, and because they love humidity and moisture, they will work great in your indoor living wall. This is especially true if this wall is near the kitchen or bathroom, as air plants love the moisture in those areas and will thrive on it.

- Don't use soil; use water for these plants.
- Mist them every couple of days or drown them in room-temperature water for half an hour every week and a half. Let them dry well before placing them on your living wall again.
- Trim dead leaves – if you find brown spots, you need to water them more often or move them around your living wall for a better spot.

Coleus

There are more than six hundred varieties of this plant, so you have most likely seen at least one type. This plant is a great addition to your living wall, no matter which variety you end up choosing, as it will add color, texture, and grandeur to your space. It is an amazingly easy, low-maintenance plant, so it's perfect for beginners. Certain varieties do very well in semi-shade, in case your living wall happens to be in a darker room. For semi-shade type of coleus, you can choose "Brilliancy," "Fishnet Stockings," "Mardi gras," or even "Japanese Giant" – make sure to ask around in your garden center if you need help finding the right variety.

- Sow the seeds about ten weeks before the last frost date. If you're planting this outdoors, make sure the temperature is higher than the normal winter temperature before moving it outside.
- Choose well-draining soil and a spot that is protected from the wind.
- Water it well and keep it moist for the first week after planting.
- If the topsoil is dry, you can water it again.

Croton

Croton is a stunning plant with shades of green, scarlet, orange, and even a few yellows thrown in the mix. It's a bushy plant and has an incredibly eye-catching texture. If you plan to grow Croton in your home, you shouldn't allow pets or children near it, as it is poisonous, including the seeds. On the other hand, croton will be a lovely addition to your living wall as it will add more depth and texture.

- Sow the seeds in well-draining soil when the temperature is over 65° F. Use a container that is large and heavy because this plant is heavy.
- Water it lightly from time to time – moisture is fine, but not wet soil.
- Croton needs sunlight, so only consider if your indoor spot has enough light during the day.
- Trim it to your liking and to prevent it from tipping over plants that are below.

Elephant Ears

Elephant ears need to be part of your living wall! They have gorgeous heart-shaped leaves with prominent veins running through them, and their color range goes from lime green to almost black. They come from tropical Asia, so they prefer moist soils and not a lot of sunlight. Once established, elephant ears get large, so make sure you trim them often and consider placing them at the bottom of your living wall.

- Plant the tuber one inch below wet soil.
- Fertilize it once a month.
- Water it at its base, so you don't get water on its leaves. Don't let the soil dry out, as the plant will struggle to survive.
- Remove brown leaves by cutting them as close to the tuber as possible.

English Ivy

Ivies are a must in any living wall. They're climbing plants, and they add a magical touch to any home. English ivy leaves are small and may vary in shape. They are not on the bushier side, but they will help cover up a few empty spots you may have in between other bigger plants. This plant would also be great in a trellis as it's very flexible and easily weaves around any frame.

- Plant it in well-draining soil.
- English Ivy needs light but not direct sunlight - if your home is too warm, it may not grow well. It needs cooler temperatures.
- Water it regularly, but only when the soil is dry to the touch.
- Trim it as needed.

Hosta

Hostas are an incredibly eclectic plant that can range from small varieties to ones three feet tall. This plant also has leaf colors in white, blue-green, and lime green, and they may be smooth or have ridges. Have your pick! Whichever variety you choose, though, hosta are breathtaking. They can also attract pollinators if your living wall is outdoors, and they bloom in summer – their flowers are also colorful!

- Place the plant's roots in well-draining soil, leaving its crown visible at the soil surface.
- Add fertilizer after planting it and use a mulch to keep it moist.
- Water it regularly – hosta need soil that is moist but not wet.
- Cut its flower stalks to encourage new growth.

Pothos

Pothos is a beginner's best friend. It won't die if it's exposed to too much or too little light. It will also tolerate too much water or too little water. Even the soil type won't affect it negatively. You will love it for how easy it will be on you. This plant is a great one for your indoor living wall as its requirements are very low, that's why it's sometimes called "Devil's Ivy": it just keeps coming back to life! On that note, be careful if you have pets or children, as this plant is poisonous.

- Plant the seeds in well-draining soil – they do not tolerate wet soil.
- Put it in a large container. If it's inside, room temperature is perfect for optimal growth. Pothos like light – but not direct sunlight.
- Water it once the soil is dry.
- Fertilize it about once a month in spring and summer.
- Trim it as needed. If it starts browning, remove those leaves and stems immediately.

Spider Plants

Spider plants are a very popular type of plant in homes because they possess a unique shade of green. They have long, thin foliage that is light green with a white line running along the center. They may bloom in summer with white flowers. They also have an air-purifying ability. It won't truly work if you only own one or two, but it's a good fact to throw in when describing your living wall.

- Sow the seeds in well-draining soil.
- Keep the plant in a bright place but away from direct sunlight.
- Water it once a week, and once fully established, water it two to three times a week, never letting its soil dry out.
- Fertilize it once a month during spring and summer.

The table below shows you the different types of plants discussed and a summary of their properties:

Plant	Sun Exposure	Soil Type	Soil pH	Bloom
Air plant	Full sun but no direct sunlight	N/A	N/A	Varies
Coleus	Full sun, Partial sun	Any	Neutral	Summer
Croton	Full sun, Partial sun	Loamy	Neutral	Varies
Elephant Ears	Part sun	Any	Neutral to Slightly Alkaline	
English Ivy	Partial sun, Shade	Loamy, sandy	Loamy, sandy	
Hosta	Shade	Loamy	Neutral	Summer
Pothos	Partial sun	Loamy, sandy	Neutral	
Spider plant	Partial sun, Shade	Loamy	Neutral	Summer, Fall, Spring

For the best results, consult the table above and match plants that work well together and require similar care or have similar growth patterns. Remember to create a fun wall to look at as you'll want to spend a lot of your time here, and others will want to spend their time relaxing next to it.

If you opt for a full hydroponic system, then remember to set it up so that each plant gets its specific watering needs met. You should also use modular containers, if possible, so you have the option of moving things around if a particular plant is not loving its spot.

In the next chapter, we'll look at what fruits you should grow in your vertical garden if you want to grow something edible and sweet.

Chapter 7: Fruit Trees for Your Vertical Garden

Imagine walking out into your backyard on a hot, sunny day, ready to water your plants, only to see a special surprise! Your first homegrown strawberry. Or maybe it's a tomato. What's important is that you can have this experience yourself. Growing your own fruit may be the smartest decision ever. You'll have an unlimited supply of fresh fruit that you grew in your very own balcony or backyard, just a few steps away. The pride that also comes from growing your own fruit is just the cherry on top of the cake.

Many types of fruit offer an excellent opportunity to dive into your new passion for gardening as many of them are very easy plants to grow. Climbing fruit plants will make it even easier for you because they thrive on vertical supports like trellises. You won't need to worry about using up what little space you have, and you'll be enjoying your vertical garden in more ways than by just looking at it. It'll become a part of your meals and family traditions.

You'll have to consider choosing the perfect location for these crops as most of them require at least half a day of sunlight. Some of them might do well in more shaded areas, but the disadvantage there is they'll yield less fruit. The soil you use is also important to think about since, for most fruits, a combination of sandy and loamy soils is ideal.

We'll discuss this further in this chapter when we look at the best fruits to grow in your vertical garden and give you the information you need to plant each of them.

Below, you'll find a list of the best fruits to grow in your vertical garden:

1. Blackberries
2. Blueberries
3. Cucumbers
4. Grapes
5. Kiwifruit
6. Melons
7. Raspberries
8. Strawberries
9. Tomatoes
10. Watermelon

Blackberries

Blackberries are one of the best fruits to grow in your vertical garden. They're easy to grow, and they're delicious! Once established, you may expect to have a great harvest every few days. The trailing kind has canes that need to be attached to a trellis for support, which makes them perfect for your vertical garden as you'll already have the support they need.

This fruit is perennial, meaning its root will survive, but its canes will die after they've borne fruit, so you'll need to prune them for new ones to grow. Wait for the temperature to rise before planting them, as doing so too early may kill the plant. If you're reading this and counting on having blackberries in just a few months, you may be disappointed to learn that they only bear fruit in the second year. If you're looking forward to harvesting this fruit, you should be aware of this rather long wait.

- Plant them no more than one inch deep in well-draining soil and water them thoroughly.
- Use a trellis or vertical support to attach all canes once they've been established.
- Use mulch all year round to help prevent weeds and retain moisture.
- Water them two to three times per week, making sure they get a total of one inch of water weekly.
- Prune canes once they've died and turned black near the soil.

Blueberries

Blueberries are also one of the easiest fruits to grow on your balcony, backyard, or garden. They have so many health benefits that you'll be missing out if you don't include them in your vertical garden. Blueberries are full of antioxidants and have vitamins C, K, and the mineral manganese. They are said to help lower blood pressure, improve memory, and reduce LDL cholesterol levels. This means that they're not only tasty but also packed with vitamins that will improve your health.

This plant likes the sunlight and needs to be protected from wind and birds who just love to eat them! They can be grown in a container, which is ideal because blueberries require acidic soil – a type that is easily mixed or found, though, so don't worry. Like blackberries, you'll have to wait to enjoy your crops as the plant doesn't bear fruit until its second year.

The best varieties to grow in containers are "Top Hat," "Pink Lemonade," and "Pink Champagne."

- Plant the blueberry bush in a well-draining, acidic soil just below the surface. Add peat moss to your soil a few months before planting to ensure it's acidic enough for optimal development. Water it thoroughly.
- Place the container in a nice, sunny spot where it's also sheltered from the wind and birds.
- Fertilize it one month after planting.
- Use mulch to retain moisture but leave the trunk of the bush clear for proper airflow.
- Water it regularly so that it receives up to two inches of water weekly.
- Prune it after about four years to stimulate growth (pruning is not needed before then).

Cucumbers

This might be surprising to hear, but cucumbers are actually fruits and not vegetables, as they grow from flowers and contain seeds. This fruit is ideally grown on a trellis, so it will be easier to harvest. Growing it on a trellis also reduces the likelihood of fungal diseases and pests.

Cucumbers love sun and water, and they will grow easily in the right conditions. Pick them regularly so as to not weigh down the plant. Another reason to pick them sooner rather than later is that they won't taste as sweet once they are large.

Vining cucumbers are the ones you should be looking for, as they are the most suited for climbing up a trellis or vertical structure. They also grow really fast, in just a few weeks. If you want to cut them to eat, pick them when they're 6 to 8 inches long, and if you want to pickle them, harvest them when they're at two inches.

- Sow seeds one inch deep into a well-draining soil rich in nutrients. You can mix in your compost before planting them.
- Place your container somewhere with full sun exposure.

- Water it regularly, as cucumbers love water – one inch per week. Using a drip irrigation system will help not to get the leaves wet. Once fruits begin forming, increase the amount of water to one gallon per week.
- Pick the fruits using a knife or clippers, cutting the stem just above the fruit. Pick them often; if you don't, the plants will stop producing fruit.

Grapes

Grapes are so versatile as a fruit that there's no way not to love them. They are an investment because they take their time to establish and require quite a bit of care, but if you love them, they will give your vertical garden a dramatic cascading effect of beautiful vines. Moreover, if taken care of properly, this plant may last for about thirty years!

Grapes love the sun and need to have good airflow. It may take three years for them to start bearing fruit, but the wait will be worth it.

- Soak the grape vine's roots in water for about three hours before planting.
- Plant grape vines in well-draining soil in an area with full sun exposure. Water it thoroughly.

• Use mulch to retain water.

• Fertilize lightly only in the second year after planting.

• Prune it when the plant is dormant after the first year. Remove the canes that are already bearing fruit to allow for new growth.

Kiwi

Kiwis are a delicious green fruit that is loved by many. Their vines can grow quite tall, so make sure you have enough space for them before you consider growing this fruit on your small balcony or indoors. Kiwis are a climbing vine, so they are a perfect addition to your vertical structure. If you live in an especially cold area but want to grow your own kiwis, you might still be able to. There are two types of this plant, and the hardy kiwi (also known as the kiwi berry) can tolerate subzero temperatures for limited periods.

If you're looking into growing a more common type of kiwi, then it's the kiwifruit you should go for. They like the sun and warmer temperatures, but you will need a male and female to produce fruit. Just like many other fruits, you'll have to wait a while before enjoying it, but the wait will be worth it.

- Plant kiwi vines in well-draining soil, just deep enough to cover the roots.
- Attach the vines to a strong vertical structure, as they need good support. Keep in mind that the weight of the fruit will break the structure if it is not sturdy enough. Water them thoroughly.
- Place them in a very sunny spot with good airflow.
- Water them regularly, making sure the roots are not consistently wet, as kiwi roots tend to rot easily.
- Fertilize in the spring after their first year.
- Prune the female vines in winter and the male ones after blooming time.
- Harvest the fruits when they are soft to the touch.

Melons

Melons are another great option for your vertical garden, even though they are heavy fruit. As with other heavy fruits, you need to ensure your vertical structure will support the weight during fruiting. They are a delicious fruit that is best enjoyed in warmer months and makes anyone with a sweet tooth happy.

This fruit loves the sun and lots of water, so you need to keep it hydrated and in a sunny spot with at least half a day of sunlight. They don't tolerate subzero temperatures but will produce fruit much faster than your berries. Many gardeners use an old t-shirt to support the weight of this fruit while it's growing to avoid any possible damage to its vines.

- Plant melons one inch deep in well-draining soil when the temperatures are no lower than 60° F, and there is no risk of frost.
- Water them regularly with up to 1.5 gallons a week, but make sure their leaves dry off well to avoid any fungal diseases. Once they start fruiting, reduce the amount of water, as melons like hot and dry weather. This should give them a sweet taste.
- Fertilize with a non-heavy nitrogen liquid fertilizer.
- Prune the ends of the vines after fruiting.
- Harvest when their rinds are a hue of yellow or when you find cracks on the stems. If you see them separate themselves from the vine, they are probably overripe; you want to pick them before they reach this point.

Raspberries

Raspberries are quite a versatile plant to grow on your balcony or small space as they are self-fertile. This means they only need one bush to produce fruit. Even though raspberries usually prefer colder temperatures, new varieties will allow gardeners to grow them even in hotter climates.

You probably know the summer-fruiting raspberries, as they are more common, but there is another type called "fall-fruiting" or "ever-bearing," which produces fruit in the fall. The summer-fruiting type produces fruit once a year, usually during the summertime, and reutilizes the same canes. However, the ever-bearing type produces berries on new canes, fruiting in fall and sometimes the following summer. They attract pollinators and will produce fruit in the second year like most berries.

- Soak raspberries roots for two hours before planting.
- Plant them in well-draining soil, leaving the crown one inch above the ground.
- Place them in a sunny spot – raspberries may also do well in semi-shade; however, they won't produce as much fruit. If you don't have a sunny

spot for them, you may consider a partially sunny spot.

• Use mulch to retain moisture and prevent weeds from appearing.

• Water it regularly – up to one inch a week from spring until harvest.

• Prune its old canes back to the ground (old canes will be the fruiting ones that have brown stems). New, green canes (also called primocanes) will be produced every year, so don't worry about cutting the old ones to the ground as you'll be stimulating new growth.

• Harvest raspberries in early summer after the first year.

Strawberries

Strawberries are one of every gardener's must-haves. They are one of the easiest fruits to grow, kids love them, and they are sweeter when you grow them yourself – not just because you grew them yourself, but because they truly are sweeter right when you pick them. They will also look beautiful on your vertical garden as they spill out of their container, covering up any unnecessary gaps.

They love the sun, and there are three types of strawberries, the most common among home gardeners being the June-bearing ones.

These fruit in June, as the name indicates, over about three weeks. Another type is the ever-bearing one, which fruits in the spring and then lightly again in the summer and again in the late summer or early fall. The third type is the day-neutral one, which produces fruits continuously if the temperature is between 35° F and 85° F. However, the harvest is inferior to the June-bearers. Like your other berries, it'll take a year for your plant to start bearing fruit.

- Plant the seeds in well-draining soil, leaving the crown exposed when the temperature is warm.
- Water it thoroughly after planting.
- Use mulch to keep it moist.
- Water it regularly – one inch per square foot per week.
- Cut off blossoms in the first year, as this encourages the plant to develop strong and healthy roots. This will lead to a better harvest in the following year.
- Harvest when ripe, usually about six weeks after blossoming, by cutting by the stem.

Tomatoes

Tomatoes are another food that most people consider a vegetable, but they are actually a fruit. Tomatoes are also a great ally to beginners are they are easy to grow, especially in a vertical garden. They love the sun and warm temperatures, and this fruit is an excellent pick for growing indoors if you place it next to a window with plenty of sunlight – they need about eight hours daily. The best thing is that it won't take you a year to see results, as tomatoes usually start bearing fruit around three months after planting, depending on the cultivar.

For a vertical garden, the bush or dwarf variety of tomatoes is the best choice, as they won't need to be staked.

- Sow seeds a quarter of an inch deep into loose, well-draining soil. If it's being planted outside, ensure the temperatures are around (or ideally above) 70° F.
- Add organic matter to your soil a couple of weeks before planting for optimal results.
- Water it generously in the first few days after planting and then about 1.2 gallons per week.
- Use mulch after a few weeks to conserve moisture.
- Fertilize it every three to four weeks, using a slow-release, low-nitrogen fertilizer.
- Harvest when tomatoes are firm to the touch.

Watermelon

Watermelons are another popular fruit amongst most people. They can be eaten raw, juiced, used in salads, and much more. Like melons, they have varieties that are suited to be grown vertically, and you may use the same system of an old t-shirt to support their weight if needed. Planting them in a spot with sunlight and good airflow is the best for them, and in just a short couple of months (maybe three), you'll be able to enjoy your first homegrown watermelons!

If you live in a colder area, you may start planting the seeds indoors three weeks before your last frost date. If you live in a warmer place and the temperatures are above 70° F, then grow them outside right away.

- Compost your soil a couple of weeks before planting.
- Plant seeds a quarter of an inch deep into well-draining soil. Use a large container to sow them in.
- Water them regularly with about two inches of water per week until they fruit. Keep the soil moist but try not to wet the leaves. Reduce the amount of water when fruiting.

- When ripening, usually over two weeks, place cardboard or straw underneath the fruit to prevent rotting.
- Harvest when ripe – they won't ripen after being picked. To see if your watermelon is ripe, thump it; if it sounds hollow, then it's good to go! Harvest by cutting by the stems close to the fruit.

The table below shows you the different fruits discussed and a summary of their requirements:

Fruit	Sun Exposure	Soil Type	Soil pH	Plant in (season)
Blackberries	Do well in semi-shade	Sandy	Acidic	Early spring
Blueberries	Do well in semi-shade	Any	Acidic	Spring or late Fall
Cucumbers	Full sun	Loamy	**Slightly Acidic to Neutral**	Early Spring
Grapes	Full sun	Any	**Slightly Acidic to Neutral**	Early Spring
Kiwifruit	Full sun	Loamy, sandy	**Slightly Acidic to Neutral**	Spring
Melons	Full sun	Loamy, sandy	**Slightly Acidic to Neutral**	Spring
Raspberries	Do well in semi-shade	Any	**Slightly Acidic to Neutral**	Early Spring
Strawberries	Full sun	Loamy	**Slightly Acidic to Neutral**	Spring
Tomatoes	Full sun	Loamy	Acidic, **Slightly Acidic to Neutral**	Spring
Watermelon	Full sun	Sandy	**Slightly Acidic to Neutral**	Spring

With this information, you will hopefully make the best decision for you and your vertical garden. Remember that care and patience are a gardener's best friends, and without them, you won't see the results you're hoping for. Even if it takes you a year or two to get your delicious fruits, if you put in the work, the wait will be worth it.

If you're not set on specific fruits because they're your favorites, try to use the table above to help you match fruits that work well together and require similar care or have similar growth patterns. This will ensure that you'll have an easier time when first planting your crops. Consider sunlight and watering needs as these will influence your crops the most. Other than that, any fruits you choose to grow will be tasty, and more importantly, they will be grown by you, which will make them extra sweet.

Fruits may not be part of your plan for a vertical garden, but what about vegetables? Going outside and getting a head of lettuce to prepare for dinner is something most people wouldn't know about, but you can do it. In Chapter 8, we'll be talking about the best veggies to plant in your vertical garden.

Chapter 8: Vertical Veggies

Growing your own vegetables is any gardener's dream. Fresh, chemical-free crops that go right to your table are the absolute best way to nourish yourself and your family. Some people believe they can never grow their own veggies because you need tons and tons of space. However, you probably know by now that this is not true. A vertical garden will allow you to feed your family right, all from the comfort of your balcony or small backyard. Growing veggies vertically means you won't have to think twice while you're at the supermarket, making sure you haven't forgotten anything for your favorite dish.

Besides possibly giving you some privacy, a vertical garden filled with vegetables will make your experience more exciting when you're ready to harvest your first-ever crop. Often, they'll be even tastier than your store-bought vegetables, so you have nothing to lose!

Refer to Chapter 4 if you need some ideas on how to DIY your vertical garden using trellises or baskets, or even plastic bottles. As long as you have large containers that will allow your vegetables to grow, you can even plant vine crops. Anything goes once you are knowledgeable and know exactly which steps you need to take to be successful.

In this chapter, we'll be looking at the best vegetables and greens to grow in your vertical garden, their characteristics, and how they should be planted. This should give you the information you need to choose the most suitable plants for your garden.

Here's a list of the best vegetables and greens to grow in your vertical garden:

1. Beans
2. Cabbage
3. Carrots
4. Garlic
5. Lettuce
6. Onions
7. Peas
8. Peppers
9. Radishes
10. Spinach

Beans

Beans are a staple in many households, so it shouldn't surprise you that they are loved and very commonly grown by gardeners. Beans are also one of the easiest plants to grow, so as a first-time gardener, you should be happy with them.

There are two types of beans: bush beans and pole beans. There are a few differences between them, and some say pole beans taste better. Bush beans might be your initial choice because they are very compact. Pole beans would be ideal for a vertical structure since they grow as climbing vines. They are also more disease-resistant, and they grow in about a month, so you don't need a lot of patience to see results.

- Sow the seeds one inch deep into well-draining soil. This should be done outdoors when the temperature is above 50° F. Use a trellis as support for the climbing vines.
- Water them regularly – about two inches of water per week. Pole beans like water, but make sure their foliage dries well after watering.
- Add mulch to the soil the keep moisture in.
- Harvest every day to encourage more growth. They should be harvested while they're still young and tender.

Cabbage

Cabbage is a well-loved and popular vegetable. Packed with vitamins, it can be added to salads, soups, or eaten with meats and bread. It's a well-rounded veggie and an easy one to grow if you provide it with the right conditions.

Cabbages do not like hot climates, so you'll have to wait for the temperature to drop to plant it. Depending on where you live, this may be around the late summertime. Making sure the soil temperature is right will make growing cabbages much easier.

- Prepare the soil by mixing it with compost a couple of weeks before planting.
- Sow the seeds 12 to 24 inches apart in well-draining soil.
- Water it regularly with up to two inches of water per week.
- If the temperatures drop below 45° F, you should consider covering them.
- Fertilize your crops after two weeks. You may also add a nitrogen fertilizer a week later.
- Harvest by cutting at the base of its head, then remove the stem and root from the soil to prevent disease.

Carrots

Carrots are also part of the family of vegetables that enjoy cooler temperatures, and they don't even mind frost. They like their soil to be loose and sandy (or loamy), and you can plant them during spring or late summer. They will take about 3 to 4 months to be ready for harvest and three weeks to germinate, so you'll need to be patient with this vegetable.

This vegetable is well-loved because it can be grown in many climates and gives you a choice between a summer or fall harvest.

- Make sure your soil is loose; no clumps should be in the way of your carrots' roots.
- Add used coffee grounds to the soil before planting.
- Sow seeds a quarter of an inch deep, four weeks before the last spring frost date for a summer harvest or ten weeks before the first fall frost for a fall harvest.
- Water it frequently. It should get one inch of water per week at the beginning and two inches once the roots start to mature.
- Use mulch to retain moisture and to protect the roots from sunlight.
- Harvest when the size is to your liking.

Garlic

You'll be happy to know that this very popular ingredient is easy to grow, and you can get started as early as September. Garlic does not like hot weather, so you'll need to plant it before the ground freezes to be able to harvest it in the summertime. It needs low temperatures, around 40° F, to grow well.

- Prepare your soil by adding compost to it before planting.
- Plant cloves two inches deep, in their upright position, in well-draining soil.
- Use mulch right up to the last frost date.
- Fertilize it in early spring and again around early May. Use a nitrogen-heavy fertilizer.
- Water it frequently – every 3 to 5 days right until June.
- Harvest by digging up the bulbs using a garden fork.

Lettuce

Lettuce is the ultimate vertical gardener's best friend. Not only will it grow quickly, but it also won't require a lot of care. Imagine getting a fresh head of lettuce from your balcony and quickly throwing together a delicious mixed salad. Plus, lettuce likes the cooler seasons, so you can start planting it even before the first frost. It loves water, so you need to keep it hydrated, but other than that, it's an excellent choice for your vertical garden.

- Prepare the soil by mixing in the organic matter about a week before planting.
- Sow the seeds a quarter of an inch deep in well-draining soil.
- Water it well after planting. Place garlic rows in between lettuce to prevent pests.
- Fertilize it about three weeks after planting.
- Water it regularly - lettuce likes its soil moist but not wet.
- Use organic mulch to help retain moisture and keep the soil temperature cool.
- Harvest heads when they've reached their full size but before maturity.

Onions

Another crop that is perfect for the colder months is the onion. Onions are versatile, and you can use them in any dish you can think of. They can also be eaten raw or cooked and even taste excellent when pickled. They are truly magnificent vegetables! They don't require a lot to grow, and you may be surprised by how quickly you'll be making dinners with your own onions.

It is advised to plant onion sets and not seeds because it is much easier to start with the onion bulbs. In just under four months, you'll see full-sized bulbs. They even tolerate frost!

- Prepare the soil by mixing compost in before planting.
- Plant onion sets one inch deep, with the pointed end up, in well-drained, loose soil.
- Fertilize them every few weeks with a nitrogen-heavy fertilizer.
- Add mulch when the bulbs start to develop.
- Water them regularly – about one inch per week.
- When you see brown on their foliage, pull the onions carefully – they'll be ready to harvest.

Peas

Peas are also an incredibly easy vegetable to grow, and planting them yourself will change your view of them forever. Store-bought peas have nothing on the homegrown ones! They taste much better and are suited to growing vertically. Children may even join in the fun and help to plant them! Peas like the sun and an airy spot.

You can choose from one of these three varieties that are perfect to use in meals: sweet peas, snow peas, or snap peas. For the climbing variety, great for your vertical garden, you can choose between snap peas or snow peas. Peas should be planted when the weather is still cool, around March or April.

• Prepare the soil by mixing in compost and mulch around the Fall.

• Sow the seeds 4 to 6 weeks before the last spring frost date, when the temperature is around 60° F.

• Water them sporadically – up to one inch of water per week.

• Peas don't need much fertilizer; however, always choose a fertilizer low in nitrogen if using one.

• Harvesting will be possible in just over a month. Pick them in the morning, gently holding the vine while pulling the pods.

Peppers

Peppers are an amazing ingredient to have in your kitchen, and they provide a lot of vitamins that we need to stay healthy. Growing them in your vertical garden will also add lots of color to it when they're maturing. They are very resistant to pests and prefer warmer temperatures. You'll have to be a little patient as they may take almost three months to be ready for harvest, but the wait will be worth it.

• Get a head start by sowing the seeds indoors ten weeks before the last spring frost date.

• Sow seeds in well-draining soil rich in organic matter.

- Transfer plants outside when the temperatures are above 65° F. Cover the soil with plastic before transferring to ensure the soil is warm enough.
- Water them regularly – up to two inches of water per week. If the weather is warm, water them every day and cover them with mulch to lower the soil's temperature and keep moisture in.
- Harvest peppers to your liking – remember they can be green, yellow, or red, depending on maturity levels. Red peppers are the sweetest ones.

Radishes

Radishes are one of the easiest vegetables to grow. They're small and a great vegetable for your vertical garden. You'll see results in no time, so they are a great vegetable for first-time gardeners who need a little extra motivation initially. You can start enjoying your radishes in just three weeks, how great is that!

They don't love hot climates, so they should be planted in spring, but they need light to grow well and become tasty. They need loose soil to allow space for the roots to develop, so you can consider mixing sand in your soil to adjust it as needed.

- Prepare the soil by mixing organic matter into it once the soil is workable.
- Sow seeds a few weeks before the last frost in well-draining, loose soil.
- Water them consistently – moisture is good, but the soil shouldn't be overly wet.
- Harvest when their roots are one inch in diameter at the soil's surface.

Spinach

This vegetable is rich in essential vitamins like A, B, and C, as well as iron, making it important in our diet. Spinach is very similar to lettuce in terms of growth requirements and can be planted in early spring, sometimes even in winter. Spinach likes cool weather and grows better if given a few weeks of that. Keep in mind that germination will not be successful if the soil is warmer than 70° F.

Spinach likes sunlight, and because its seeds are difficult to transplant, you should plant it in its home right from the start. However, due to its growing requirements, you can start as early as the fall if where you live does not have very cold winters. If the temperature drops, you may consider covering it.

- Prepare the soil by mixing compost into it a week before planting.
- Plant seeds half an inch deep, covering them lightly with well-draining soil.
- Water them thoroughly after planting and continue to water them regularly afterward.
- Use mulch to retain moisture.
- Fertilizing spinach is not necessary.
- Harvest when spinach leaves have reached your preferred size.

Refer to the table below to find a compact list of these vegetables' requirements for optimal growth:

Veggie or Green	Sun Exposure	Soil Type	Soil pH
Beans	Full sun	Any	Neutral
Cabbage	Full sun	Loamy	Neutral
Carrots	Part sun	Loamy, sandy	Neutral
Garlic	Full sun	Loamy, sandy, clay	Neutral
Lettuce	Full sun, Part sun	Loamy, sandy	Neutral
Onions	Full sun	Any	Slightly Acidic to Neutral
Peas	Full sun, Part sun	Loamy, sandy	Slightly Acidic to Neutral
Peppers	Full sun	Loamy	Slightly Acidic to Neutral
Radishes	Full sun, Part sun	Sandy	Neutral
Spinach	Full sun, Part sun	Sandy	Neutral to Slightly Alkaline

Now you have the knowledge you need to make the best decision in terms of what vegetables to include in your vertical garden. Imagine how happy you'll be when you see your first crop turn into your next meal. They may need time and a few adjustments, but that will not stop you.

If you don't have time to grow vegetables or you are not particularly fond of them, then the next chapter may have the answers you've been looking for. A green wall does not have to be just green, it can be as colorful as you'd like, and growing flowers on a living wall just makes it more fun. Read the next chapter to find out more about how to grow flowers on a living wall.

Chapter 9: Growing Flowers on a Living Wall

If you don't feel the need to grow your own crops, it doesn't mean that a vertical garden or living wall isn't for you. As we've seen , you can choose a green wall where none of your plants are edible. You can go for a little more color and add flowers to your vertical space. Flowers can create such a statement out of any blank wall or space in your home, both indoors and outdoors. They catch everyone's attention, and the scents they release may just fill your home with the most natural perfumes.

You can choose flowers that are perennials for a year-round colorful wall. However, if you feel like switching things up, you can always switch containers. Modular containers would be particularly good in this scenario as you can change them regularly or even have others ready for different seasons. It's completely up to you to decide what works best in your space and home. Colors, scents, practicality, and ease of watering are all things to consider when creating your very own living wall.

In this chapter, you'll find information related to the best flowers for a living wall or vertical garden, their characteristics, and their requirements.

This is a list of the best flowers and greens to plant in your vertical garden or living wall:

1. Aurina, or Basket of Gold
2. Clematis
3. Climbing Hydrangea
4. Climbing Rose
5. Creeping Phlox
6. Snow-in-Summer
7. Trumpet Vine
8. Wisteria

Perennials are defined as any plant that lives for more than two years. They are traditionally lower maintenance than annuals, but they do have their requirements to thrive. Keep reading to learn how to grow your perennials in your garden!

Aurinia, or Basket of Gold

This flower has a stunning yellow color and blooms in spring. It has beautiful gray/blue/green foliage for the rest of the year. It's a low-growing perennial that will cascade down your living wall.

Aurinia is drought resistant, loves the sun, and attracts pollinators. It is very easy to maintain this type of flower, and it'll do well even if you don't do much to it – just leave it be, and it'll look great.

- Plant seeds in well-draining soil. Water well after planting.
- Place it in a sunny spot with some daily shade and water it once a week.
- Fertilize it every few weeks.
- Shear it after flowering for a better-looking result.

Clematis

This flower is also an easy one to maintain. It has many varieties with different colors, so you can choose whichever one you think will look best on your living wall. They are considered a vining, climbing plant, but they will cascade down when placed on the top row of your wall.

Most of its varieties bloom in the early spring and again in the fall.

Clematis like sunlight and nutrient-rich soil. You'll need to place it somewhere it will get proper air circulation.

- Prepare the soil by adding compost to it before planting.
- Sow the seeds in well-draining soil.
- Water it regularly with one inch of water per week.

- Use mulch to retain moisture and keep the soil cool.
- Prune clematis once a year for a neat appearance.

Climbing Hydrangea

This flower needs a little more patience to reach its full potential, as it may take from two to five years to reach maturity. Once it does, it's a breathtaking sight. It's a bushy flower with dark green leaves and beautiful, delicate white flowers that bloom in the spring and summertime. They also produce an incredible scent when blooming and, in the fall, the flower heads turn a beautiful red/brown color that suits the season so well.

Climbing hydrangeas prefer partial shade. They may tolerate some sun exposure, but they'll need to be watered more often if that's the case.

- Prepare the soil by adding compost before planting.
- Sow seeds one inch deep into well-draining soil.
- Water them with at least one inch of water per week – climbing hydrangeas like their soil moist but not overly wet. If the temperature rises, water more often.

• Apply mulch to help retain moisture.

• Fertilize them once in the spring before blooming.

Climbing Rose

There's nothing wrong with choosing a more common yet beloved flower for your vertical structure. Roses are timeless, and climbing roses are stunning flowers that will be admired all year long. There are plenty of varieties to choose from: hybrid tea roses, bourbons, English roses, and more. Choose your favorite, and you'll have a flower on your living wall that will last for years.

• Plant seeds in well-draining soil.

• Water them regularly – daily when the weather is hot.

• Apply mulch in the Fall.

• Fertilize them in the Spring.

• They'll need pruning after a few years after planting.

•

Creeping Phlox

This flower is a beautiful, carpet-like perennial with five-pointed flowers which come in many different colors. It's a cascading type of flower, so it will cover up any spaces you have in your living wall. It's an easy flower to grow as it doesn't require a lot of care or knowledge. After blooming, its stems turn woody, and you should remove them to encourage new growth that will bloom again. It also attracts pollinators, which is great for the entire wall.

Creeping phlox loves the sun and adapts easily to any type of soil. It will thrive if given enough light and doesn't need much more.

- Plant it at the soil level, not burying the stem, in well-draining soil.
- Water it regularly until established. During hot periods, water it more often.
- Fertilize it in early spring.
- Cut stems back after blooming to encourage more flowers to grow.

Snow-in-Summer

This flower gets its name from its appearance and the time of year at which it blooms. It blooms in early summertime, covering the ground with beautiful white flowers that look like snow.

This flower spreads easily, so if you're planting it in your living wall, it is recommended to contain it to where you want it using individual containers. To be certain to avoid spread, you may also cut off its stems right after flowering.

Snow-in-summer likes the sun and should be planted in the early spring. It will adapt to most soils if they are well-drained but might be more successful in sandy soil that is not rich in nutrients. It will tolerate short periods of drought.

- Sow seeds in a (very) well-draining soil.
- Water it sparsely.
- There is no need to fertilize this flower.
- Prune older blooms every year to keep them looking neat.

Trumpet Vine

This flower is a showstopper! It has beautiful orange and burnt-orange tube-shaped flowers that really stand out against its dark green leaves. If you're a bird lover, then you'll probably want to make this a must on your living wall because trumpet vines attract hummingbirds! However, many gardeners wouldn't recommend growing this flower because it's a fast-growth one. It can easily take over other plants and grow up to forty feet in a single season! So, if you decide to plant it in your living wall in a container, you might have a better chance at keeping it under control. Pruning it often is recommended.

Trumpet vine should be planted in the spring or early fall. It likes sunlight and will produce the best flowers when it has at least half a day of light.

- Plant seeds in well-draining soil.
- Watering is not usually needed and should only be done if there are clear signs of wilting.
- No fertilizer is recommended due to its aggressive growth.
- Prune it regularly and pull out any new shoots you find.

Be careful if you decide to plant this flower, as every part of it is poisonous if ingested or if it touches your skin.

Wisteria

Even though it is a gorgeous vining flower, Wisteria is aggressive in its growth, much like the trumpet vine. They can easily crowd out other plants, and you shouldn't grow them near your home. Some varieties are non-invasive such as the Amethyst Falls Wisteria, so consider this type if you really want to plant it against a wall in your home.

Wisteria blooms lavender flowers in the spring and should be planted in early spring or fall. They take a long time to fully mature, so it is advised to buy established plants instead. They like the sun and fertile, moist soil.

- Plant established plants in well-draining soil.
- Apply mulch to retain moisture and prevent weeds.
- Water the plant if it hasn't rained that week.
- Prune it twice a year – in late winter and during the summer for a more controlled, neat-looking vine.

In the tables below, you'll find a summary of these flowers' requirements for easier comparison between them. They are divided into two tables: one for vining flowers, the other for cascading flowers.

Vining Flowers

Flower	Sun Exposure	Soil Type	Soil pH	Bloom	Perennial
Climbing Hydrangea	Partial shade	Loamy	Slightly Acidic	Spring, Summer	Yes
Climbing Rose	Full sun, Part sun	Loamy	Neutral	Late Spring to early Fall	Yes
Trumpet Vine	Full sun, Part sun	Any	Neutral to Acidic	Summer	Yes
Wisteria	Full sun, Part sun	Any	Slightly Acidic to Neutral	Spring	Yes

Cascading Flowers

Flower	Sun Exposure	Soil Type	Soil pH	Bloom	Perennial
Aurina	Full sun	Chalky, sandy, loamy	Neutral to Alkaline	Spring	Yes
Clematis	Full sun, Part sun	Loamy	Varies according to the variety chosen	Varies according to the variety chosen	Yes
Creeping Phlox	Full sun, Part sun	Any	Neutral	Mid-Spring, Summer	Yes
Snow-in-Summer	Full sun	Sandy	Neutral	Early summer	Yes

As you can see, the options are endless, and it's up to you and your creativity to turn your living wall into your favorite space. You can match colors or go with a less traditional route and use flowers that clash. Use a mix of sun-loving flowers on the top rows and place those that prefer shade on the lower rows. You can even go with only one type of flower if you want! It's your living wall; it's your time, effort, and patience, so you're the only one who can make these decisions. Turning your living wall into something you love will ensure you spend a lot of time taking care of it, not because you have to, but because you love it.

You may now be wondering how to take care of these plants, flowers, vegetables, or fruits. In the next chapter, we talk about how to control weeds, pests, and disease, so that you know what to do if any of these problems arise.

Chapter 10: Controlling Weeds, Diseases, and Pests

Making your own vertical garden or living wall is not all fun and games. The positive aspect is that you will end up with a breathtaking space that will help you relax and improve your life.

However, besides the care and patience, you have to give your vertically grown space, you also have to think about weeds, diseases, and pests. It's not the glamorous side of things, but it is a factor you have to deal with sooner or later, and I strongly recommend that you handle it as soon as possible.

Controlling weeds, diseases, and pests is not only an issue for in-ground gardeners. Soil, water, and other factors may lead to these problems, and you will need to think about how you want to solve these issues. As always, planning ahead will ensure you have the means and knowledge to get ahead of whatever problem you may face and eradicate it quickly.

You may think that using pesticides will solve all your problems, but they may not always be the solution you should be going for. What things should you consider when controlling weeds, diseases, and pests? What problems can arise, and how do you fix them? Let's dive into it.

What Contributes to Weeds, Diseases, and Pests?

Some of the things that may affect your plants and contribute to weeds, diseases, and pests are imbalanced soil, watering, and pesticides. That's right; sometimes, in trying to fight off the problem, you're only adding to it by using pesticides.

Insects like moths, butterflies, and other small insects like to chew on your damaged plants. You may find yellow spots on the leaves of your plants which indicate that tiny insects are around. Of course, you don't want insects eating away at your crops, but you may be creating another problem by eliminating this issue with pesticides. This is especially true when gardeners use a general insecticide, not knowing which insect is chewing their plants. This may cause another problem because a general insecticide will also kill off the insects that may be beneficial to your plants. You need to understand that harmful insects are present because of a damaged plant; they don't feed off healthy ones. In other words, they are not the root cause of the problem. They are a symptom of it, and you should be addressing the actual cause by looking into why your plant is damaged.

If your plants have a disease, then it may be biotic or abiotic. Like the name indicates, biotic diseases are caused by living organisms and abiotic by non-living agents like herbicides, pollution, or nutrients. Once again, these diseases may appear due to an imbalance in the soil, which will be more likely to get attacked by insects. There are certain insects like leafhoppers that may also spread diseases when feeding. But we know there is a root problem that needs to be addressed first: soil, water, plant damage. These are most likely to be the causes of weeds, diseases, and pests.

What Issues Should You Pay Attention To?

Issues in a living wall or vertical garden are similar to general issues any gardener finds in their garden. The main difference is that a vertical garden is likely to have fewer diseases and pests because the soil used is controlled. Using drip irrigation systems will also help with root rot and overwatering problems because it's a slow, precise system. But this doesn't mean that issues won't appear, so paying attention to your plants and living wall is worth it.

In vertical gardens or living walls, the most common issues are over-or-underwatering, sunlight/shade, imbalance of soil, and plant diseases. It is important to identify the issue quickly before your entire wall or garden is affected.

Watering Needs

Even though it's easy to find out the watering needs of a plant, most gardeners tend to water their plants a little too heavily, which leads to all sorts of problems. Making sure you do not overwater your plants is Rule Number One of keeping a beautiful, healthy vertical garden or living wall.

You can try using an automated drip irrigation system so that the task is automated or double-check every time to see if the soil is ready for more watering before you do it. Stick to your plant's schedule, and you should be fine.

A sign that you may be overwatering your plants is if the leaves wilt or turn yellow. You may also see mold on top of the soil, or the stem may feel soft to the touch. If these signs are occurring, do not panic; just stop watering your plant for a few days. Let the plant regain its energy, and make sure the soil is fully dry before you start watering it again. You may also re-pot the entire plant, but if you let it breathe and your space has good air circulation, the plant will have a fighting chance.

If you're not overwatering, you may be underwatering your plants. Even though this is less common, it sometimes happens among new gardeners. The signs of underwatering are different from overwatering because the plants won't be getting the nutrients they need. They may experience slow growth, their leaves' edges may be turning brown and start to curl, they won't have any blossoms, and their stems will be brittle and crisp. Underwatering is just as bad as overwatering. You will still be harming your plants, so make sure you follow a strict watering schedule and respect your plants' needs.

Sunlight vs. Shade

Most plants need light to help them grow, so you have to give them that light. Once again, each plant is different and will have slightly different needs. Getting too little or too much light will result in an unhealthy-looking vertical garden or living wall.

Respect the instructions on how to handle your plant. If a plant requires 6-8 hours of light daily and your chosen location doesn't allow for this, then you need to move it somewhere else or avoid buying that plant in the first place. It's just a headache you want to avoid.

If your plants' leaves are falling off or growing lanky, this is a sign of an unhealthy plant. This plant needs more light. If the leaves are crunchy or you find scorched spots on them, then your plant is probably receiving too much light.

Light exposure is important for your plants, and it is something you can fix. However, it would be simpler if you think about this aspect before buying a certain type of plant that isn't suitable for the location you have in mind for it.

Imbalanced Soil

In Chapter 3, we talk about the importance of soil mixtures, types, and pH levels. Every plant is different and may need adjustments, and if you're not providing these, your plants will not flourish. For example, soil that is not well-draining affects the plants' roots, stems, and leaves. It will harm your plants, and you won't even be able to see that at first.

Check drainage before planting by watering your soil and seeing if there's water escaping your container. You don't want to find it all because that would imply your plant won't be getting enough nutrients, but there needs to be *some* drainage. Checking before planting is the easiest way to avoid problems in the future.

Pests and Plant Diseases

Even though there is a lower risk because of controlled soil, water systems, and the structure being off the ground, vertical gardens may still suffer from pests and diseases. These are more difficult to solve than overwatering, for example, but there are solutions available. Some of them may even be found in your pantry.

If you find out your vertical structure has a pest or disease problem, here's how you can deal with that issue.

How to Control or Deal with these Problems:

The first and obvious answer to this is prevention. Prevention is an easier way to get healthy, tasty crops than solving your problems later on. Healthy plants are not likely to get diseases or pests. By ensuring your soil is the right mix for your plants, using the right compost and mulch, removing old leaves, weeds, and following the instructions given for your specific plant, you are taking the necessary steps to prevent pests and disease from appearing.

Even rotating plants will help with prevention. Even if it seems like it will take longer to get your vertical garden set up, it will help you in the long run. If you still encounter a problem even after having done this, this is how you should handle it:

- **Investigate the Situation**

You do not want to act before identifying which pest or disease is attacking your plant, so investigate first. Give yourself time to find the root cause of the problem so that your solution will be effective and the least dangerous to your plant.

- **Give It Time**

Give your plant time to fix the problem on its own. If not seriously damaged, your plant or other plants nearby may help you fix the problem themselves. Nature is just that incredible, and if you allow it some time, maybe you won't have to take any actions. Some insects, for example, may come to the rescue and eat the disease away. Other plants may overtake the sickly ones so that you just have to remove the damaged ones. Give it time.

- **A Kind Solution**

If you must take matters into your own hands, go with the solution that is kind to the environment, to your plants, and to you. There are so many ways around it that you really don't have to go running for the chemical pesticides to solve your problems. Mulching helps with weeds, for example. You can even buy beneficial bugs at a store. The goal is not to reach for a chemical pesticide immediately but to think before you act.

With that said, sometimes, there *is* a need for a pesticide. However, the solution is to make your own, so you are fully aware of what's in it. You will find below three DIY pesticides that are kind to the environment.

1. Neem Oil

This oil is a great option when dealing with pests and diseases in plants. It'll affect chewing insects but not pollinators, which your plants always need. You can use it as a spray or add it directly to the soil when you have young plants – the oil will seep through the soil, the plants will absorb it, and once insects chew on them, they will die off. To make it into a spray, this is what you will need:

- 2 teaspoons of neem oil
- 1 teaspoon of liquid soap
- 8.5 ounces of water

Mix in the three ingredients, pour them into a spray bottle and shake it well. Then spray the mixture onto the leaves (top and bottom), ensuring they are well soaked in the product. Spray them early morning or in the evening when they are not facing direct sunlight.

This mixture will help with mealybugs, whiteflies, aphids, and even root rot and black spots.

2. Baking Soda

Baking soda is known for its dozens of uses around the house, so it's no surprise that it can also help you in the garden. This ingredient is present in most households and is an effective one in treating black spots. This is what you'll need:

- 4 teaspoons of baking soda
- 1 teaspoon of mild liquid soap
- 10 oz of water

Mix the three ingredients well, pour them into a spray bottle, and shake it well. Then spray the mixture onto the leaves, making sure you cover both sides. Continue shaking the spray so that it doesn't separate. Ensure you cover the entire plant, including shoots and new leaves, even if it doesn't seem like they're infected. This mixture will help with black-spot and white mildew.

3. Used Coffee Grounds and Crushed Eggshells

This DIY is not much of a DIY as it is just two ingredients that you should add to your plants that will create a barrier for insects. Used coffee grounds and crushed eggshells will deter some insects from attacking your plants, and these two household items can be found in any home. Plus, it's almost as if you're composting or recycling, so bonus points for that!

Used coffee grounds – these have a much lower pH, so they're better to mix in with the soil. You can sprinkle some on top of the soil or mix them lightly into the soil. Coffee grounds stop ants and other chewing insects from coming onto your plants.

Crushed eggshells – this household ingredient is high in calcium carbonate, which deters slugs and snails from climbing your plants. Any other ingredients also high in calcium carbonate would help, but crushed eggshells are sharp, which is another advantage to using them.

Whether they are simple or complex, dealing with issues in your vertical garden or living wall is daunting for many first-time gardeners, so you're not alone in feeling that way. Use the above methods and procedures to help you solve your gardening issues, and you will soon find your plants looking happy and healthy again. The most important step is the first one, to have control.

If you're observant, you will detect a problem quickly and be able to fix it just as quickly.

You're right at the end of your journey into becoming a vertical garden or living wall connoisseur; you're ready to get your hands dirty! Let's look at a checklist of everything you'll need from the start of your journey until the end - well, maybe until the middle; this book won't give you recipes to teach you what to do with your fruits and vegetables after you harvest them.

Chapter 11: Your Vertical Gardening Checklist

This chapter will look at a final checklist of everything you need for a vertical garden or living wall. This is it; you're ready to start on your path to becoming a vertical gardener. You have studied and learned how to start this journey from scratch. It's been a long, daunting road, full of information and tips on making this first time a successful one, but you should be confident that you have the tools you need to make it on your own.

If you've forgotten what steps are the most important to consider when starting your vertical garden or living wall, do not worry. What you'll find below is a detailed list of these steps that will put you on the right path and lead you to the finish line. Use the checklist at the end of the chapter to make sure you haven't forgotten anything, and tick off each step as you go along.

Steps to Take for Your Vertical Garden or Living Wall

Which Structure to Choose?

You know by now that the first step is to decide if you want a vertical garden or living wall and which type of support you'll choose for your base. Will you go for a trellis or a more DIY approach? The type of vertical structure you choose will be important for finding out what types of plants you can grow. Moreover, deciding on the type of support early on will make it easier to design it the way you want.

Do you want a luscious green wall or some pops of color peeking through by adding flowers? Do you want a tiered system so you can easily install a drip irrigation system? Or maybe you prefer the contrast between nature and concrete and want to plant your green plants and flowers in cinder blocks. Or you can go for a simple, farmhouse style with mason jars and a wood plank right in your kitchen for easy reach.

Thinking ahead allows you to plan the design of your vertical garden or living wall. This is especially important if you're trying to catch people's attention by creating intricate shapes and details on your wall. Certain designs will allow a hydroponic system to be installed, and others won't. So planning ahead will give you the flexibility to choose and change your mind before anything's done.

Materials and Hardware

You need to think about which materials you'll need to add to your wall or the structure you may be building. You may need wood to build a few boxes or a ladder. You may need hooks to hang your containers from. You will most likely need to waterproof your wall with paint, plastic, or other materials to ensure that it doesn't get damaged by the humidity.

Getting the materials all at once will save you the headache of going back and forth to the store. Decide on the support system you want, write a list of all the materials and hardware you'll need to build it or add onto it, and you're set for a perfect start.

Location

The wall or location you choose for your vertical structure is important because of the light that reaches it, the air circulation it has, and ultimately, the plants you will be able to pick. If you have certain types of plants in mind, then you might have to be more flexible with the location you choose for your vertical garden or living wall. However, if you're set on a spot, you need to be more flexible with your choice of plants. This is especially true for those living in small apartments with a tiny balcony or a small amount of available space. You want to make sure to choose somewhere you'll love having a green wall, but also somewhere where it works.

Getting to know the placement of your vertical structure before choosing your plants will set you on the right track for growing healthy, lush plants.

Which Plants to Pick

Having figured out where your vertical garden or living wall will be set up is key to selecting your plants correctly. You'll know how many hours of light you have during the day or if you need strong plants that can withstand wind.

Picking plants may seem daunting, but it can be made simpler by answering the question: will you want them to be edible or not? If yes, you should focus on vegetables and fruits that you can grow in the same vertical garden. But, if you answer no, then it's all about the plants and flowers you love that are also suited for the space you've selected.

Different Soils for Plants' Specifications

The soil is the home of every plant. Sticking to your plants' specifications is key for a good start when taking care of them. If a plant needs clay soil and you put it in a loamy one, your plant won't thrive. The same goes for drainage issues: if your soil is not adapted to your plants' needs, you'll be facing root rot, diseases, and unhealthy plants.

It's important to read about your plants to find the best soil match for each one of them. Refer to Chapter 3 for a more detailed and thorough look into the soil types and specifications if you need help with this.

Watering Method

Do you have time to water your plants a few times a week? Will you stop yourself from overwatering them? Do you have the budget to incorporate an automated irrigation system into your vertical structure? These are questions that will help you decide which watering method you should use for your vertical garden or living wall.

Contrary to popular belief, living walls can be watered manually. They don't all need a sophisticated hydroponic system to grow well and be healthy. It may take you more time to water them manually, but it will be easier on your pockets.

The watering system you choose will directly affect your vertical garden or living wall, so choose wisely and take your time to reflect on what works best for you. Look again at Chapters 2 and 5 if you want more information on irrigation systems and how to make your own.

Fertilizers

Thinking about the soil and water won't be enough to help your plants grow healthy but considering your fertilizer options will help the process. Fertilizers may be added at the moment of planting and during the growth period. Sometimes, if the soil drains a little too well, nutrients won't be absorbed by the plants. Adding fertilizers and mulching will help your plants tremendously.

Read about your plant's specifications to discover which nutrients they need the most and make sure they get them. You should think about whether you want to add chemicals to your plants or not. If you don't want to add chemicals, think of ways to use organic matter or natural solutions to give your plants what they need.

Environmentally Friendly DIYs

Thinking ahead of the potential problems that may arise is intelligent because you'll be ready to solve them if they happen. Considering your options to control weeds, pests, and diseases before you find them will give you a better chance of helping your plants survive. The easiest route is to buy a pesticide from the store, but as you may remember, in Chapter 10, we talked about how you can fix different issues with nonchemical homemade products, most of which are in your pantry.

It is smart to be prepared because even if you do not need to spray your plants down with some pesticide, you will feel confident that you haven't overlooked anything and are ready for whatever may come.

Garden Tools

You will need gardening tools to work on your vertical gardening when harvesting and pruning, and taking care of your plants in general. Getting them right at the start will ensure you have everything you may need before you need it. This way, you won't have to waste valuable time getting them later.

Eventually, you will most likely need a few tools, so consider buying pruning shears, a garden fork and a trowel, a spade, gloves, loppers, a watering can (if applicable,) and maybe a hoe and a rake if you have a large garden space. Getting the tools right from the start will help the process along.

To recap, this is the final vertical gardening checklist:
- Vertical structure
- Materials and hardware
- Location
- Which plants to pick
- Different soils for plants' specifications
- Watering method
- Fertilizers

- Environmentally friendly DIYs
- Garden tools

Once you've ticked off each step, you'll know you're ready to start. I know it has been a long road, but you are now ready for whatever may come. With the right tools and knowledge, your plants will be beautiful and healthy, and you'll be able to enjoy them soon. In the next and final chapter, we'll discuss the final precautions and considerations one should make before going into vertical gardening.

Chapter 12: Final Precautions and Considerations

Growing your own garden without compromising floor space is the only option for many homeowners. Vertical gardens and living walls hit the mark by taking up little space and giving new gardeners the option of having their own green paradise on their tiny balcony or small backyard or even inside their home.

Creating a living wall will also allow you to be more creative and hands-on throughout the entire process. However, this may not be for everyone, and there are many things to consider before diving into this new world. Obviously, you want to make the best decision for you, your budget, and even your free time, so having a clear goal and detailed plan is paramount for a successful vertical garden. In this chapter, we'll look at the pros and cons of having your own vertical garden or living wall, which will hopefully help you make the final decision.

Pros and Cons to Consider

Pros

Space Saver

Not everyone has a lot of empty space in their home or garden to plant their favorite crops; therefore, a vertical garden or living wall will provide you with the same option while being a space saver. The fact that these gardens grow up (and down) and not out allows you to grow up to five times more than traditional horizontal gardening, so you only need enough height to grow your favorite plants.

An Art Installation

Besides having a practical side, a vertical garden or living wall can be absolutely stunning, making it seem almost like an art installation rather than just a garden. If you plan which types of plants and the colors you'll mix and match, your vertical structure will say a lot more than "I'm here to feed you." A tall, lush green wall welcomes any customer or guest into space in the best way possible.

Creativity

Creating your own vertical garden or living wall will make you use your creativity. That is the beauty of these gardens as well. If this is a passion project and you're a creative person, you'll soon realize you can be very artistic with this space. You can plan which materials, plants, and colors you want to add to your vertical structure. You may even need to be creative when choosing which structure to utilize.

More Variety

Because the plants outlined in this book grow upwards, you may grow a wide variety of plants that you otherwise wouldn't be able to. Having a vertical structure with individual pockets will allow you to grow many varieties of plants or vegetables and herbs that would take up a large amount of space in a more traditional garden.

Privacy

Besides being aesthetically pleasing, vertical gardens and living walls may also help you by giving you some privacy or creating a cover from a busy road or nearby neighbors. It's a natural and beautiful way to add a little more intimacy to your balcony or yard without breaking the bank or creating an eyesore for your neighbors.

Easier for Beginners

A vertical garden or living wall is an easier option for beginners. The amount of care the plants will need is much less when compared to traditional gardening methods. Some vertical gardens or living walls do not even use soil, so the potential problems that arise with most crops wouldn't be a problem here. This is a smart and easy choice for a beginner.

Mobility

Due to modular containers and, most likely, smaller containers, mobility is one of the biggest pros of vertical gardens and living walls. You'll be able to move things around and switch them up as needed. Moreover, while maintaining them, you won't have to bend over for hours or hurt your knees in the process because everything is vertical. This is a major factor to consider, especially when one reaches a certain age.

No Clutter

Having potted plants is great, but when you have various vases and containers scattered all over the place, it can create a very messy, cluttered look. Having a vertical structure with all your pots or containers on a single wall will make the place look neater. In this case, you can even have different containers because once your plants grow and start hanging down, you won't see them anyway.

Noise-Reducing

A vertical garden and living wall can help with your concentration and productivity. They act as noise-reducing barriers and would make a great addition to an open-plan office space or even an apartment located in a busy area. Block out the sound of traffic by installing your own green wall.

Stress Relief

These vertical structures will positively affect your health, and one of the ways they can do that is by acting as a stress reliever. Studies conducted by Alan Ewert and Yun Chang have shown that being surrounded by a green, natural environment lowers your heart rate, blood pressure, and general stress in a matter of minutes. In a world where everything rushes by at 100 miles a minute, having something that helps you calm down during the day is beneficial.

Recycling

Another positive aspect of creating your vertical garden or living wall is the potential for recycling. If making it yourself, you'll be able to reuse materials you have lying around your home, such as plastic water bottles or even containers you no longer need. You'll be contributing to a greener world not just literally but also through the choices of materials and tools you use.

Cons

Not Enough Space for Roots

By having plants too close to each other or in smaller containers, your plant's roots won't have a lot of space to grow. This need not be a huge issue, but it will most likely translate into smaller crops. In a traditional garden, you leave more space between crops for proper growth, and roots have all the space they need to grow.

Dry Out

The problem with vertical gardens or living walls is that the top plants may dry out quicker than they normally would had they been planted in the ground. Due to the weather, airflow, and sunlight, plants on top rows may dry out. A solution for this is to move your plants occasionally.

Sun Blockers

Just as the top plants might fry out, they may also block other plants from getting sunlight. Because they'll grow and cascade over the edges of their containers, the top rows of plants may overshadow the ones underneath them, blocking any light from reaching them. The solution to this is the same as the previous one; rotate your crops regularly. Getting modular containers is the key to streamlining this process.

Expensive

Even though there are a few hacks, tips, and tricks you can use to make your own vertical structure, it can still be quite expensive. If you add up the cost of materials, soil, irrigation systems, plants, and tools you'll need in the long run, this project can become quite expensive. This can be helped with some careful planning before you purchase any items. Look for cheaper options and reusing materials. However, if you decide to buy a ready-made vertical structure, it can be quite pricey.

Messy

Unfortunately, this has to be said: vertical gardens and living walls can be really messy. Dirt may fall off from containers, water splashes everywhere, and leaves fall. All of these things are normal and will happen. This won't be a big deal in a traditional garden, but when growing against a wall on a balcony, you may have to constantly clean your floor. A tray at the bottom of the structure will help but will not entirely prevent it from happening.

Humidity

Another problem is caused by having water near or against a wall. If not properly prepared and insulated, humidity and mold will appear and may damage your wall. This is not ideal, and you don't want to have to deal with mold later on. So make sure you prepare your wall correctly and check on it from time to time to detect any problems early on.

More Maintenance

Even though you won't have to deal with as many weeds or certain issues that are more common in traditional gardens, there is substantial maintenance to keep up with when it comes to vertical gardens and living walls. Plants living in these containers will need constant care. They will need regular pruning and trimming, careful and calculated addition of nutrients, and even adjusted watering methods. You will also need to be more vigilant. But, because it won't be a large structure, you won't have to spend all your free time taking care of it.

No Support for Heavier Crops

The most common vertical gardens won't be sturdy enough for certain heavy crops like melons and squashes, even if they can grow vertically. Making sure you have the right support for whatever you're growing is important to avoid damage when the plants start fruiting.

These are the pros and cons in a simple, easy to remember list:

Pros	Cons
Space saver	Not enough root space
An art installation	Dry out
Creativity	Sun blockers
Grow more variety	Expensive
Privacy	Messy
Easier for beginners	Humidity
Mobility	More maintenance
No clutter	No support for heavier crops
Noise-reduction	
Stress relief	
Recycling	

These are the main pros and cons of building a vertical garden or living wall, but another big question that you should ask yourself is, "Is this sustainable?"

Is a Vertical Garden or Living Wall Sustainable?

When thinking about this question, you can think of two things: is this sustainable for you? And is this a sustainable, environmentally friendly structure?

For starters, a green wall is a new, modern way of achieving sustainability in buildings where environmentally friendly foundations were not considered at the time of building. A green wall may be added later to the bland, concrete building and provide many health benefits for its tenants and owners. Moreover, installing a green wall in your business may translate into more sales and draw people's attention. This may lead to financial growth, which is positive for any business, but is it sustainable? Will you choose to have a green wall because of its benefits if, in the end, it could cause more problems?

Is a green wall sustainable for you? Is the time and effort you have to allot to it sustainable in the long term? Everyone is enamored with the idea of a green wall these days, but many don't consider its risks. This is a structure that requires time, effort, money, and attention. If you're not capable of giving it the right amount of these things, this is not a sustainable idea for you, and you should re-consider it.

Reflecting on whether building it yourself or buying a ready-made vertical structure is about more than that initial effort and time it'll take you to get it up and running. This is a commitment, maybe not for life but for a long time, that should be taken seriously, and if you don't think you're ready for it, you should assess those feelings.

However, if you're excited about this new step but maybe feeling a little nervous, that is normal. It's like when you start a new job or move to a new city, it may be nerve-wracking at first, but you can do it! With the right guidelines and help, you can achieve anything you put your mind to! Your very own vertical garden or living wall is just a few steps away, and you should be excited for this new journey you're about to embark on. It's going to be a fun one!

Conclusion

We hope this book has been useful to you. This started as a vertical gardening beginner's guide to growing fruit, vegetables, herbs, or flowers on a vertical structure. However, you should feel more confident than a beginner by now. You have learned the basics of vertical gardening, including how to plant crops and plants, so your journey should feel easier.

Good luck with creating your first vertical garden or living wall – you can do this!

Here's another book by Dion Rosser that you might like

References

3 signs your green wall is in trouble [and what to do about it]. (n.d.). Retrieved from Growupgreenwalls.com website: https://growupgreenwalls.com/blogs/growupdates/3-signs-your-green-wall-is-in-trouble-and-what-to-do-about-it

Albert, S. (2015, June 8). 10 natural, organic steps to control garden pests and diseases. Retrieved from Harvesttotable.com website: https://harvesttotable.com/10-natural-organic-steps-to-control-garden-pests-and-diseases/

Amber. (2018, December 29). The 15 best perennials for A vertical garden - garden tabs. Retrieved from Gardentabs.com website: https://gardentabs.com/best-perennials-vertical-garden/

Andrychowicz, A. (2019, March 25). The amazing benefits of vertical gardening. Retrieved from Getbusygardening.com website: https://getbusygardening.com/vertical-gardening-benefits

Aurinia saxatilis (Basket-of-Gold). (n.d.). Retrieved from Gardenia.net website: https://www.gardenia.net/plant/aurinia-saxatilis-basket-of-gold

BBC Gardeners' World Magazine. (2019, July 5). Plants for a living wall. Retrieved from Gardenersworld.com website: https://www.gardenersworld.com/plants/plants-for-a-living-wall/

Benefits of outdoor living green walls and vertical gardens. (2017, October 19). Retrieved from Biotecture.uk.com website: https://www.biotecture.uk.com/benefits/benefits-of-exterior-living-walls/

Best plants for vertical gardens. (2016, May 4). Retrieved from Balconygardenweb.com website: https://balconygardenweb.com/best-plants-for-vertical-garden-vertical-garden-plants/

Best Vining fruits and vegetables for vertical gardens. (n.d.). Retrieved from Davesgarden.com website: https://davesgarden.com/guides/articles/best-vining-fruits-and-vegetables-for-vertical-gardens

Brougham, R. (2018, February 12). 14 Inspiring DIY Flower Walls. Retrieved from Familyhandyman.com website: https://www.familyhandyman.com/list/14-inspiring-diy-flower-walls/

Dian. (2019, July 10). Getting started vertical gardening: Tools you'll need. Retrieved from Dianfarmer.com website: https://dianfarmer.com/getting-started-vertical-gardening-tools-youll-need/

Drip Irrigation for Living Walls. (2018, March 29). Retrieved from Plantsonwalls.com website: https://www.plantsonwalls.com/guides/drip-irrigation-living-walls/

Dyer, M. H. (2018, July 10). The upsides and downsides of vertical gardening. Retrieved from Gardeningknowhow.com website: https://blog.gardeningknowhow.com/gardening-pros-cons/vertical-gardening-pros-and-cons-2/

Editors, R. S. (2015, July 1). Everything you need to know to grow your own vertical garden. Retrieved from Realsimple.com website: https://www.realsimple.com/home-organizing/gardening/how-to-make-a-vertical-garden

Garden Design Magazine. (2015, July 14). 12 garden tools to buy - essentials for beginners - garden design. Retrieved from Gardendesign.com website: https://www.gardendesign.com/how-to/tools.html

Home Improvement Pages Australia. (n.d.). Choosing irrigation systems for vertical gardens. Retrieved from Com.au website: https://hipages.com.au/article/choosing_irrigation_systems_for_vertical_gardens

Horticulture Landscaping: Vertical Gardening. (n.d.). Retrieved from Tnau.ac.in website: https://agritech.tnau.ac.in/horticulture/horti_Landscaping_vertical%20gardening.html

How to start a vertical garden today. (2018, March 6). Retrieved from Growingorganic.com website: https://growingorganic.com/diy-guide/how-to-start-a-vertical-garden/

Justin. (2019, February 1). Vertical gardening pros and cons - garden tabs. Retrieved from Gardentabs.com website: https://gardentabs.com/pros-cons/

Kinetic Design-http://www. kinetic. co. (n.d.). How to grow herbs in A vertical garden. Retrieved from Com.au website: https://www.baileysfertiliser.com.au/gardening-blog/guide-to-growing-herbs-in-a-vertical-garden

Lafreniere, A. (2019, December 11). Living wall pest control. Retrieved from Planthardware.com website: https://planthardware.com/living-wall-pest-control/

Levin, A. (2017, July 18). How to design and install a living wall. Retrieved from Fesmag.com website: https://fesmag.com/topics/trends/14894-how-to-design-and-install-a-living-wall

Living Wall Systems. (n.d.). Retrieved from Ansgroupglobal.com website: https://www.ansgroupglobal.com/living-wall

Lowin, R., & SanSone, A. E. (2018, March 3). 35 DIY vertical garden ideas to show off your green thumb. Retrieved from Countryliving.com website: https://www.countryliving.com/gardening/garden-ideas/how-to/g1274/how-to-plant-a-vertical-garden

Magyar, C. (2020, April 17). 10 fruits and veggies to grow vertically for epic yields in tiny spaces. Retrieved from Ruralsprout.com website: https://www.ruralsprout.com/grow-food-vertically/

Martin, K. (2021, February 12). 12 climbing fruit plants. Retrieved from Urbangardengal.com website: https://www.urbangardengal.com/climbing-fruit-plants/

Metson, E. (2019, August 28). Are living walls worth creating over other sustainable options? Retrieved from Biofriendlyplanet.com website: https://biofriendlyplanet.com/green-alternatives/sustainable/are-living-walls-worth-creating-over-other-sustainable-options/

Natasha. (2016, January 11). 12 ideas which materials to use to make A vertical garden. Retrieved from Fantasticviewpoint.com website: http://www.fantasticviewpoint.com/12-ideas-materials-use-make-vertical-garden/

Natural Pest & Weed Control. (n.d.). Retrieved from Savingwater.org website: https://www.savingwater.org/lawn-garden/natural-pest-weed-control/

Natural remedies for pest, disease, and weed control. (2020). Elsevier.

Nichols, M. R. (2018, March 1). Green walls are great, but they need to work efficiently. Retrieved from Inhabitat.com website: https://inhabitat.com/green-walls-are-great-but-they-need-to-work-efficiently/

Old Farmer's Almanac. (n.d.). Growing Guides. Retrieved from Almanac.com website: https://www.almanac.com/gardening/growing-guides

Osmond, C. (n.d.). 56 of the best vertical gardening ideas: #27 is gorgeous! Retrieved from Backyardboss.net website: https://www.backyardboss.net/best-vertical-gardening-ideas

Planting guide. (2018, May 18). Retrieved from Livewall.com website: https://livewall.com/plant-selection/planting-guide/

Plants & Flowers. (n.d.). Retrieved from Thespruce.com website: https://www.thespruce.com/plants-and-flowers-5092674

Poindexter, J. (2018, April 17). How to start a DIY vertical garden (and 7 ideas you should try). Retrieved from Morningchores.com website: https://morningchores.com/vertical-garden/

Pot, S. (2018, August 21). What is the best soil for fruit trees? Retrieved from Springpot.com website: https://www.springpot.com/best-soil-for-fruit-trees/

Pros and cons of vertical gardens. (2013, April 10). Retrieved from Easyverticalgardening.com website: https://easyverticalgardening.com/types-of-vertical-gardens/pros-and-cons-of-vertical-gardens/

Search, plants - BBC gardeners' world magazine. (n.d.). Retrieved from Gardenersworld.com website: https://www.gardenersworld.com/search/plants/

Smith, A., & Clapp, L. (2021, March 24). How to make a living wall – an easy step by step to DIY your own living wall system. Retrieved from Realhomes.com website: https://www.realhomes.com/advice/how-to-create-a-living-wall

Sood, G. (2019, April 11). Indoor vertical garden: How to grow & things to consider. Retrieved from Homecrux.com website: https://www.homecrux.com/indoor-vertical-garden/120830/

The Daily Gardener. (2020, July 27). 7 easy steps to construct a perfect vertical garden. Retrieved from Thedailygardener.com website: https://www.thedailygardener.com/construct-vertical-garden

The planter box approach to green walls. (2018, October 5). Retrieved from Com.au website: https://www.tensile.com.au/the-planter-box-approach-to-green-walls/

The pros and cons of a living wall. (n.d.). Retrieved from Calibre-furniture.co.uk website: https://www.calibre-furniture.co.uk/blog/the-pros-and-cons-of-a-living-wall

Tilley, N. (2007, July 13). Growing A vertical vegetable garden. Retrieved from Gardeningknowhow.com website: https://www.gardeningknowhow.com/edible/vegetables/vgen/growing-a-vertical-vegetable-garden.htm

Tirelli, G. (2019, April 2). Top 10 benefits of living green walls or vertical. Retrieved from Ecobnb.com website: https://ecobnb.com/blog/2019/04/living-green-walls-benefits/

TOP 10 Plants for Vertical Garden. (2017, June 6). Retrieved from Nurserylive.com website: https://wiki.nurserylive.com/t/top-10-plants-for-vertical-garden/2172

Ultimate Guide to Living Green Walls. (n.d.). Retrieved from Ambius.com website: https://www.ambius.com/green-walls/ultimate-guide-to-living-green-walls/

Vertical goodness: 10 DIY living walls kits for green living. (2017, August 8). Retrieved from Decoist.com website: https://www.decoist.com/diy-living-walls-kits/

What Are Vertical Gardens? (n.d.). Retrieved from Ambius.com website: https://www.ambius.com/green-walls/what-are-vertical-gardens

What foods can I grow in a vertical garden? (2018, August 14). Retrieved from Livewall.com website: https://livewall.com/faq-items/what-foods-can-i-grow-in-a-vertical-garden/

What Herbs grow best in a vertical garden? (2019, February 8). Retrieved from Easyverticalgardening.com website: https://easyverticalgardening.com/what-herbs-grow-best-in-a-vertical-garden/

Ewert, A., & Chang, Y. (2018). Levels of nature and stress response. *Behavioral Sciences, 8*(5). doi:10.3390/bs8050049

Almanac, O. F. (n.d.). *Container Gardening with Vegetables*. Old Farmer's Almanac. https://www.almanac.com/content/container-gardening-vegetables

Container Gardening vegetables that grow in containers. (n.d.). Texas A&M AgriLife Extension Service. Retrieved from https://agrilifeextension.tamu.edu/solutions/container-gardening/

https://www.facebook.com/thespruceofficial. (2018). *Learn the Basics of Hydroponics: the Most Efficient Gardening Method*. The Spruce. https://www.thespruce.com/beginners-guide-to-hydroponics-1939215

https://www.facebook.com/thespruceofficial. (2019). *Here's How to Grow Delicious Veggies In Containers*. The Spruce. https://www.thespruce.com/vegetable-container-gardening-for-beginners-848161

5 Reasons You Should Start Indoor Gardening. (2019, December 17). Retrieved from Houseandhomestead.com website: https://houseandhomestead.com/5-reasons-you-should-start-indoor-gardening/,

10 indoor fruit trees you can grow at home year-round. (2021, January 11). Retrieved from Bobvila.com website: https://www.bobvila.com/slideshow/10-indoor-fruit-trees-you-can-grow-at-home-year-round-578652

12 best herbs to grow indoors. (2019, August 3). Retrieved from Balconygardenweb.com website: https://balconygardenweb.com/best-herbs-to-grow-indoors-indoor-herbs/

12 unique indoor plants with personality & traits. (2020, July 22). Retrieved from Balconygardenweb.com website: https://balconygardenweb.com/unique-indoor-plants-with-houseplant-traits/

Asthon, D. (2019, July 25). 21 awesome indoor garden ideas for wannabe gardeners in small spaces. Retrieved from Demiandashton.org website: https://demiandashton.org/indoor-garden-ideas/

Beginner's guide to indoor gardening. (2018, May 17). Retrieved from Backtotheroots.com website: https://blog.backtotheroots.com/2018/05/17/beginners-guide-to-indoor-gardening/

Carlson, R. E. (2019, September 30). 15 fun and easy indoor herb garden ideas. Retrieved from Homesteading.com website: https://homesteading.com/indoor-herb-garden-ideas/

Clark, J. (2019, June 10). 17 easiest vegetables to grow indoors for a harvest all year -. Retrieved from Tipsbulletin.com website: https://www.tipsbulletin.com/growing-vegetables-indoors/

Coelho, S. (2019, February 28). The beginner's guide to getting started with indoor gardening. Retrieved from Morningchores.com website: https://morningchores.com/indoor-gardening/

Courtney, P. (2020, August 9). 6 reasons to start growing an indoor garden. Retrieved from Optimisticmommy.com website: https://optimisticmommy.com/6-reasons-to-start-growing-an-indoor-garden/

Euan. (2020, April 15). 7 surprisingly easy fruits to grow indoors. Retrieved from Greenthumbplanet.com website: https://greenthumbplanet.com/easy-fruits-to-grow-indoors/

Fruits & Vegetables That Grow Well Indoors. (2012, November 12). Retrieved from Sfgate.com website: https://homeguides.sfgate.com/fruits-vegetables-grow-well-indoors-51958.html

Gomez, J. (2020, June 14). 20 best indoor flowering plants that are easy to grow indoors. Retrieved from Womenshealthmag.com website: https://www.womenshealthmag.com/life/g32843710/best-indoor-flowering-plants/

Indoor garden design ideas - 10 great options - indoor gardening. (2019, July 5). Retrieved from Indoorgardening.com website: https://indoorgardening.com/10-indoor-garden-design-ideas-to-inspire-you/

ION. (2015, March 30). 5 factors to consider to set up an indoor garden. Retrieved from Designlike.com website: https://designlike.com/5-factors-to-consider-to-set-up-an-indoor-garden/

Ionescu, F. (2020, May 6). 50 astonishing indoor garden ideas [with pictures] - YHMAG. Retrieved from Youhadmeatgardening.com website: https://youhadmeatgardening.com/indoor-garden-ideas/

Jones, N. (2019, November 25). 51 of the best indoor garden ideas for this year - A nest with A yard. Retrieved from Anestwithayard.com website: https://anestwithayard.com/indoor-garden-ideas

Lane, J. (2017, June 25). How to grow indoor fruits, vegetables & herbs. Retrieved from 104Homestead.com website: https://104homestead.com/how-to-grow-food-indoors/

Neveln, V. (2016, March 15). 22 of the most beautiful blooming houseplants you can grow. Retrieved from Bhg.com website: https://www.bhg.com/gardening/houseplants/projects/blooming-houseplants/

Peters, J., Garcia, I., & Morgan, B. (2018, January 24). 17 indoor herb gardens that will add New Life to your kitchen. Retrieved from Housebeautiful.com website: https://www.housebeautiful.com/lifestyle/gardening/g1877/indoor-herb-gardens/

Poindexter, J. (2017, January 31). 24 newbie-friendly vegetables you can easily grow indoors. Retrieved from Morningchores.com website: https://morningchores.com/growing-vegetable-indoors/

Postconsumers Content Team. (2014, May 27). 10 herbs and vegetables (and a fruit) that are easy to grow indoors. Retrieved from Postconsumers.com website: https://www.postconsumers.com/2014/05/27/grow-indoor-vegetables/

Rhoades, H. (2009, October 30). Houseplant maintenance: Basic tips for indoor houseplant care. Retrieved from Gardeningknowhow.com website: https://www.gardeningknowhow.com/houseplants/hpgen/basic-care-of-houseplants.htm

Sheehan, L. (2019, November 25). 15 rare and unusual houseplants to grow. Retrieved from Ruralsprout.com website: https://www.ruralsprout.com/unusual-houseplants/

Sood, G. (2019, April 11). Indoor vertical garden: How to grow & things to consider. Retrieved from Homecrux.com website: https://www.homecrux.com/indoor-vertical-garden/120830/

The Best Ways to Take Care of a Potted Herb Garden. (2012, April 28). Retrieved from Sfgate.com website: https://homeguides.sfgate.com/ways-care-potted-herb-garden-26463.html

The Editors. (2018, May 15). Spice up your dinner with these herbs you can grow indoors year-round. Retrieved from Goodhousekeeping.com website: https://www.goodhousekeeping.com/home/gardening/a20705923/indoor-herb-garden/

Trivedi, K. (2019, November 7). Gardening Tips: Indoor plants care and maintenance guidelines. Retrieved from Republic World website: https://www.republicworld.com/lifestyle/home/gardening-tips-indoor-plants-care-and-maintenance-guidelines.html

Wright, A. (n.d.). 15 perfect indoor garden design ideas for fresh houses. Retrieved from Sawhd.com website: https://sawhd.com/indoor-garden-design-for-easy-and-cheap-home-ideas/

(N.d.-a). Retrieved from Everydayhealth.com website: https://www.everydayhealth.com/healthy-home/reasons-to-start-a-garden.aspx, (N.d.-b). Retrieved from Well.org website: https://well.org/gardening/create-your-own-indoor-garden-guide/

Printed in Great Britain
by Amazon